Lady Bird

Examining the ideas, philosophies and strategies that inform and enable a young woman's self-determination for a new century, this is a detailed, insightful study of Greta Gerwig's much-loved, influential and critically acclaimed film.

Drawing on Transcendentalism, French feminist thought, Californian art and the work of iconic American essayist Joan Didion, Rob Stone approaches *Lady Bird* as a film about young women's self-determination in relation to other women and waves of feminist history. Structured to emulate the evolving conscience and emerging consciousness of the film's eponymous protagonist, this new volume in the *Cinema and Youth Cultures* series provides an incisive portrait of a particular American youth subculture struggling to assert its identity between the shock of 9/11 in 2001 and the global financial crisis of 2008. It also sensitively examines tensions between Gerwig and Lady Bird, and between *Lady Bird* being set in 2002 and made in 2017. Written by an expert on American independent cinema and the dynamics of World Cinema, this volume explores strategies of self-determination that ignite in the friction between mothers and daughters and culminate in considerations of how the film's form and aesthetics lead to reflections on its philosophy and politics.

Situating *Lady Bird* in the genre of youth movies and feminist film practice and culture, this book is ideal for students and researchers looking at wider dialogues and discourses about feminism, philosophy, gender, genre and American independent filmmaking.

Rob Stone is Professor of Film Studies at the University of Birmingham. His research is on World cinema, American independent cinema and Hispanic cinemas. He is the author of *Walk, Don't Run: The Cinema of Richard Linklater*.

Cinema and Youth Cultures
Series Editors: Siân Lincoln and Yannis Tzioumakis

Cinema and Youth Cultures engages with well-known youth films from American cinema as well as the cinemas of other countries. Using a variety of methodological and critical approaches the series volumes provide informed accounts of how young people have been represented in film, while also exploring the ways in which young people engage with films made for and about them. In doing this, the Cinema and Youth Cultures series contributes to important and long-standing debates about youth cultures, how these are mobilized and articulated in influential film texts and the impact that these texts have had on popular culture at large.

The Motorcycle Diaries
Youth, Travel and Politics in Latin America
Nadia Lie

Lady Bird
Self-Determination for a New Century
Rob Stone

Mustang
Translating Willful Youth
Elif AKÇALI, Cüneyt ÇAKIRLAR, Özlem GÜÇLÜ

Mary Poppins
Radical Elevation in the 1960s
Leslie H. Abramson

For more information about this series, please visit: https://www.routledge.com/Cinema-and-Youth-Cultures/book-series/CYC

Lady Bird

Self-Determination for a New Century

Rob Stone

LONDON AND NEW YORK

First published 2023
by Routledge
4 Park Square, Milton Park, Abingdon, Oxon OX14 4RN

and by Routledge
605 Third Avenue, New York, NY 10158

Routledge is an imprint of the Taylor & Francis Group, an informa business

British Library Cataloguing-in-Publication Data
A catalogue record for this book is available from the British Library

ISBN: 978-1-032-14748-2 (hbk)
ISBN: 978-1-032-14749-9 (pbk)
ISBN: 978-1-003-24090-7 (ebk)

DOI: 10.4324/9781003240907

Typeset in Times New Roman
by KnowledgeWorks Global Ltd.

Contents

	List of Figures	vi
	Series Editors' Introduction	viii
	Acknowledgements	x
	Introduction	1
1	Mothers and Daughters: Genealogy and Simultaneity	5
2	Class and Classes: Education and Consciousness	34
3	Love and Attention: Aesthetics and Feelings	60
4	Acts and Gestures: Verticality and Transcendence	87
	Bibliography	113
	Index	121

Figures

1.1 Lady Bird reaches for the symbolic order 13
1.2 Opening shot: mother and daughter facing but not seeing each other 18
1.3 Marion interposing the handmade object of a dress between herself and her daughter 20
1.4 Mother and daughter regard themselves and each other in a mirror 21
1.5 One of Marion's many unsent letters reveals her true feelings about her daughter 23
1.6 Lady Bird subscribes to a Derridean process of becoming 28
2.1 Lady Bird as a non-Catholic pupil in a Catholic school 40
2.2 Lady Bird cites Kant and denounces dogma in a special assembly on abortion 43
2.3 Lady Bird in the chorus of Sondheim's *Merrily We Roll Along* 59
3.1 'Is it *too* pink?' An inter-generational contest of colours 61
3.2 Lady Bird wishing she could live through something 63
3.3 A holdover from grunge and a punk throwback… 67
3.4 …with a touch of *Annie Hall* 68
3.5 Lady Bird performs self-determination on the flat canvas of Sacramento 70
3.6 Saoirse Ronan as Christine 'Lady Bird' McPherson 82
3.7 Golden hour shots of the hand-me-down geography of Sacramento… 85
3.8 …are shared by Lady Bird and Marion 85
4.1 Lady Bird as superhero alter ego 93

4.2 Lady Bird reveals her superhero alias: 'It's given. To me by me' 94
4.3 Lady Bird builds on her Derridean process of becoming by leaving the crossed-out name of an ex-boyfriend next to that of her new one 106
4.4 Lady Bird enacts a vital stage in her Derridean process of self-determination by putting herself under erasure 107
4.5 Their last hurrah: Lady Bird and Julie at prom 107
4.6 Match-cuts of mother… 110
4.7 … and daughter create rapturous simultaneity 111
4.8 'It's me. Christine' 111

Series Editors' Introduction

Despite the high visibility of youth films in the global media marketplace, especially since the 1980s when Conglomerate Hollywood realised that such films were not only strong box office performers but also the starting point for ancillary sales in other media markets as well as for franchise building, academic studies that focused specifically on such films were slow to materialise. Arguably the most important factor behind academia's reluctance to engage with youth films was a (then) widespread perception within the Film and Media Studies communities that such films held little cultural value and significance, and therefore were not worthy of serious scholarly research and examination. Just like the young subjects they represented, whose interests and cultural practices have been routinely deemed transitional and transitory, so were the films that represented them perceived as fleeting and easily digestible, destined to be forgotten quickly, as soon as the next youth film arrived in cinema screens a week later.

Under these circumstances, and despite a small number of pioneering studies in the 1980s and early 1990s, the field of 'youth film studies' did not really start blossoming and attracting significant scholarly attention until the 2000s and in combination with similar developments in cognate areas such as 'girl studies.' However, because of the paucity of material in the previous decades, the majority of these new studies in the 2000s focused primarily on charting the field and therefore steered clear of long, in-depth examinations of youth films or was exemplified by edited collections that chose particular films to highlight certain issues to the detriment of others. In other words, despite providing often wonderfully rich accounts of youth cultures as these have been captured by key films, these studies could not have possibly dedicated sufficient space to engage with more than just a few key aspects of youth films.

In more recent (post-2010) years, a number of academic studies started delimiting their focus and therefore providing more space for in-depth examinations of key types of youth films, such as slasher films and biker films or examining youth films in particular historical periods. From that point on, it was a matter of time for the first publications that focused exclusively on key youth films from a number of perspectives to appear (*Mamma Mia! The Movie*, *Twilight* and *Dirty Dancing* are among the first films to receive this treatment). Conceived primarily as edited collections, these studies provided a multifaceted analysis of these films, focusing on such issues as the politics of representing youth, the stylistic and narrative choices that characterise these films and the extent to which they are representative of a youth cinema, the ways these films address their audiences, the ways youth audiences engage with these films, the films' industrial location and other relevant issues.

It is within this increasingly maturing and expanding academic environment that the **Cinema and Youth Cultures** volumes arrive, aiming to consolidate existing knowledge, provide new perspectives, apply innovative methodological approaches, offer sustained and in-depth analyses of key films and therefore become the 'go to' resource for students and scholars interested in theoretically informed, authoritative accounts of youth cultures in film. As editors, we have tried to be as inclusive as possible in our selection of key examples of youth films by commissioning volumes on films that span the history of cinema, including the silent film era; that portray contemporary youth cultures as well as ones associated with particular historical periods; that represent examples of mainstream and independent cinema; that originate in American cinema and the cinemas of other nations; that attracted significant critical attention and commercial success during their initial release and that were 'rediscovered' after an unpromising initial critical reception. Together these volumes are going to advance youth film studies while also being able to offer extremely detailed examinations of films that are now considered significant contributions to cinema and our cultural life more broadly.

We hope readers will enjoy the series.

Siân Lincoln and Yannis Tzioumakis
Cinema and Youth Cultures Series Editors

Acknowledgements

Lady Bird (Gerwig 2017) struck me as marvellously intricate and meaningful from the moment the fledgling Lady Bird bailed from her mother's car. It embodies much that I find fascinating, innovative and empathetic in American independent cinema. That said, my misgivings about writing a book on girlhood were deep and genuine and I am very grateful to my splendid colleagues Cat Lester, Alaina Schempp and Christina Wilkins for answering all my questions. Special thanks too to all the undergraduate students who offered brilliant insights into Lady Bird in my all-time favourite seminars. Luis Freijo, Jimmy Hay, Andy Henderson and Deborah Shaw provided incisive feedback on early drafts and Andrea Sofía Reguiera Martín shared her thesis, for which I am most grateful. Special thanks to Deborah and series editor Yannis Tzioumakis for kindly convincing me to write this book, and to Natalie Foster, who made space for it in the Cinema and Youth Cultures series. More than ever, thanks to Esther Santamaría Iglesias, who co-watched every film and series with me and kept me focused while keeping herself well. To you this book is given. By me to you.

Notes on the text and complementary video essays

All the dialogue and script directions cited are from the *Lady Bird Screenplay Book* (Gerwig 2021) in the A24 screenplay collection. Script directions are italicised throughout. All films and series have their director and year of release, and all characters have their actor, on first mention.

Three video essays by the author illustrate and explain the philosophies underpinning *Lady Bird* that are explored in this book and may be freely accessed online:

The Lady Bird Book of Derrida: https://vimeo.com/741410157
The Lady Bird Book of Kant: https://vimeo.com/743882955
The Lady Bird Book of Irigaray: https://vimeo.com/751183043

Introduction

The American teenager is no longer an angry young man, not Holden Caulfield nor James Dean. She is smart, maybe not booksmart but certain she is smarter than most people, which is why tact seeps out of sentences she should probably think through first. She might be/could be/can be pretty but isn't 'lovely' and anyway this is not what defines her. She has friends but they tend to irritate her; if they were cooler, she would be too. She has some okay teachers and some who ignore her potential, which is already burdened by the lower class and income of her parents, not to mention patriarchy. When she thinks about it, which is often, adolescence is one big dumpster fire and school is the accelerant. She fully intends to write some of these thoughts down. She was assigned *Little Women* one school year and read it again last summer. She has *The Vagina Monologues* on order at the public library because her school refuses to stock it and even then she had to stare down the librarian. She watches, pays attention and waits for something important to happen after the interval called adolescence: a sweet and sticky space between childhood and adulthood like bubble gum stretched between her forefinger and teeth. Meet her and she extends a hand to shake, aiming for sophistication, managing to be blunt.

'Christine?'

As soon as she has a hold on her clumsiness she will make a grand Romantic gesture.

'Lady Bird!'
'Is that your given name?'
'Yes.'
'Why is it in quotes?'
'I gave it to myself. It's given. To me by me.'

DOI: 10.4324/9781003240907-1

Self-Determination for a New Century

Released worldwide in 2017 by A24, *Lady Bird* was produced by IAC Films and Scott Rudin Productions. It displayed its independent credentials by having its premiere at the Telluride Film Festival in September, then moving to the Toronto International Film Festival a week later and the New York Film Festival in October, before going wide in November with the European release in February 2018. Grossing over $50 million in the United States and Canada, *Lady Bird* amassed more than $80 million worldwide and five Academy Award nominations in January 2018 for Best Film, Best Director and Best Original Screenplay for Greta Gerwig, Best Actress for Saoirse Ronan and Best Supporting Actress for Laurie Metcalfe. It made the annual ten best lists of the National Board of Review and the American Film Institute as well as coming second on those of *IndieWire, The A.V. Club* and *Time.* Most importantly, it keeps coming up in seminars with my students at the University of Birmingham in the United Kingdom, for whom it is a favourite film of the kind that prompts an exclamation of love and a warning not to say anything bad about it because Saoirse Ronan is SO good, Greta Gerwig's script is BRILLIANT and the mother-daughter relationship especially is just like...at which point words tend to fail those who offer a throaty growl of recognition instead. That *Lady Bird* might resonate with and thereby represent a particular youth culture of smart young women, who have leapt from school to university and are holding onto the film for balance, is less in doubt than the sense of worth its members can sometimes have about themselves. Influential and relatable, *Lady Bird* played a key role in the self-determination of several of these students, including one who adopted dyed red hair before coming out as non-binary. They're doing fine.

This book arises from questions of self-determination that start with the tensions between mothers and daughters and continue through matters of gender, class, race, income, religion, education and politics, prompting considerations of how the film's form and aesthetics lead to reflections on its philosophy and politics. Its aim is to present *Lady Bird* as a work of curiosity and unusual focus that is grounded in an exceptional screenplay, direction, aesthetic, performances and both the period 2002–03 that it depicts and the time of its release in 2017. It is important to note, for example, that Christine 'Lady Bird' McPherson (Saoirse Ronan) is not only coming of age in America at the start of a new century but also between the two events that will define her generation: the attack on the

World Trade Centre on 11 September 2001 and the financial crisis of 2008. Thus, while *Lady Bird* describes the typical dismissiveness and putative rebellion of a smart, white, low-income, young woman, whose solipsism means she takes every setback personally, it simultaneously skewers a post-9/11 culture that was not the fault of youth, even though they would inherit its debt in the financial crash of 2008 and the social ruptures that followed. Already too late for something and, at the same time, too early for anything at all, *Lady Bird* takes place in the interval between 9/11 and the start of something beyond its pall, tracking the self-determination of a teenager who finds herself between the rock of home and the hard place of anywhere else.

Chapter 1 – 'Mothers and Daughters: Genealogy and Simultaneity' – asks who speaks for the smart girls and maps an inter-generational dialogue between those who do. It explores two lines of female genealogy: the extrinsic, which is handed down through various waves of feminism, and the intrinsic, which is defined by simultaneity in the relationship between Lady Bird and her mother. It contends that *Lady Bird* pushes away from the majority of films about youth cultures that emphasise hormonal behaviours, physical attractiveness and consumerist desires in order to describe a youth culture that is low-income, female, smart and curious, sarcastic and conscious of irony, and engaged in deliberate means of betterment and escape. And it reveals how the film's subversion of the conventions of the coming-of-age genre gives way to forceful, feminist intent. Chapter 2 – 'Class and Classes: Education and Consciousness' – contends with the complexities of society and education that contextualise *Lady Bird* as well as related matters of gender, politics, faith, class, consciousness, income and race in representations of adolescence. It situates *Lady Bird* at a crucial time in recent American history, with the trauma of 9/11 and the war in Iraq all impacting on youth culture. And it scrutinises the autobiographical elements that Gerwig downplays, particularly her Catholic schooldays in Sacramento, while also considering *Lady Bird* in relation to the #MeToo movement that accompanied the film's release.

Chapter 3 – 'Love and Attention: Aesthetics and Feelings' – examines the aesthetic realm of *Lady Bird* and finds it responsive to the film's ethos that love and attention are the same thing, which emerges from Transcendentalism and the mystic Simone Weil. It explores the influence of Joan Didion and how the film's palette honours Wayne Thiebaud's paintings of Sacramento. Paying attention to texture, colour, costume and music, this chapter also examines the rituals of high school, the obvious and unlikely things that spark enduring memories, and the songs that capture and release such moments. Finally, Chapter 4 – 'Acts and Gestures: Verticality and Transcendence' – tracks the evolution of thought from Transcendentalism down through the ideas of Simone Weil and Joan Didion to *Lady Bird*, which is posited as Greta Gerwig's treatise on self-determination. This philosophical thread, which is informed by Luce Irigaray's ideas of verticality, describes a practice of self-reliance that is intuitive and individualistic but bound to the creation of a community or culture that is also considered in terms of the various film genres that have recently focused on female coming-of-age stories. The book therefore concludes by examining Lady Bird's capacity for empathy and allyship, reading her grand Romantic gestures as evidence of Lady Bird as a work in progress on her way to self-determination for a new century.

1 Mothers and Daughters

Genealogy and Simultaneity

Lady Bird is both birdlike and ladylike. A liminal being, her existence at the end of girlhood and on the cusp of womanhood is similarly in-between. Indeed, bearing in mind that she is Lady Bird (avian) and not Ladybird (insect) reminds us that the spaces in-between things are important. Historically, she comes of age between the third and fourth waves of feminism; too late to be a Riot Grrrl and too early for the Internet. Aged seventeen and in-between, she embodies the words to 'I'm Not A Girl, Not Yet A Woman' by Britney Spears, which was released in January 2002, a few months before the events of *Lady Bird*; but she walks to school with Alanis Morissette's anthemic 'Hand in My Pocket' on the soundtrack instead and channels her resentment of everything into performing Stephen Sondheim's show tune 'Everybody Says Don't' (1964) when she gets there. Unsurprisingly, there is a great deal of stress and apprehension around Lady Bird, whose introspection and performative gestures create accordion-like tensions between generations that are enacted in *Lady Bird* at the mother-daughter level in terms of their similarities and differences, and thematically too, in the context of overlapping waves of feminism.

Rights and Declarations

There are three, maybe four, waves of feminism that are relevant to *Lady Bird*. Then again, the wave metaphor might misnomer a succession of manifestos and movements that foreground and fight for female-centred rights. In 18th-century France, Olympe de Gouges linked women's rights to abolitionism and wrote *Declaration of the Rights of Woman and of the Female Citizen* (1791), which was published a year before Mary Wollstonecraft's *A Vindication of the Rights of Woman: With Strictures on Political and Moral Subjects* (1792). Both works influenced the 1848 Seneca Falls Convention in the United

DOI: 10.4324/9781003240907-2

States that gave rise to the American suffragette movement and its *Declaration of Rights and Sentiments* (1848), which held that 'the history of mankind is a history of repeated injuries and usurpation on the part of man toward woman, having in direct object the establishment of an absolute tyranny over her' (Halsall 1998). The declaration thus asserted that 'because women do feel themselves aggrieved, oppressed, and fraudulently deprived of their most sacred rights, we insist that they have immediate admission to all the rights and privileges which belong to them as citizens of these United States' (ibid.). But the Seneca Falls Convention did not unite all women because no Black women were invited to attend and the campaign for universal suffrage proved secondary to the demand for white women to have the vote as a recalibration of their status from beneath Black men, who had been awarded the right to vote by the 14th Amendment to the Constitution in 1868 (Staples 2018). Consequently, this first wave ebbed in 1920 when the 19th Amendment granting women the right to vote was deemed by many to be an end in itself despite the continuing lack of rights of Black women, whose suffrage would remain impeded in numerous social and economic ways.

In 19th-century America, the reformist Margaret Fuller allied her feminism to Transcendentalism and wrote *Woman in the Nineteenth Century* (1845), a foundational American feminist text (see Marshall 2013). This was a major influence on the activist Susan B. Anthony, who cofounded with Elizabeth Cady Stanton several feminist organisations and newspapers in the late 19th century and whose suffragism changed the ways and means of organising thought and action in the cause of women's rights. By the second-wave feminism of the 1960s, however, when their names would be invoked in the naming of the Stanton-Anthony brigade of the New York Radical Feminists, splinter groups had diverged from the common ideological basis for feminist activism and revealed fault-lines that recalled the racial divisions of Seneca Falls. Boosted and yet diluted by the civil rights and anti-Vietnam War movements, second-wave feminism became not only more radical but also more theoretical in its conceptualisation of a utopia that posited gender as a social construct and opposed the two-headed beast of capitalism and patriarchy. Equal pay, birth control, credit cards for women and the ruling in Roe v. Wade were a series of achievements linked to this second wave that encountered such resistance in mainstream media that many young women in the 1980s hesitated to ally themselves with the stereotype of angry man-haters. This meant that feminism, which advocates women's rights on the basis of equality between all people, could be hurled and received as an insult.

By the third-wave feminism of the early 1990s, which is relevant to Lady Bird's formative adolescence, feminism was more centred on the potential of youth than the resentment of middle-age. Third-wave feminism is a debated and divisive term, however, bound up in personal narratives that explore violence and abuse against women as lived-in feminist theory in works like Eve Ensler's *The Vagina Monologues*, which was first performed in 1996 and published in 1998. Such works raised awareness but could seem elitist and remote, lacking correspondence with the everyday burden of being a teenager like Lady Bird, who is convinced that her life is boring and, therefore, that she might have nothing to add or say. Part of the problem is the generation gap between the second and third waves of feminism, between those who grew up with feminism as a white, middle class construct and those who sought to apply feminist theory to a much wider range of people. In this respect, the mother-daughter relationship in *Lady Bird* suggests the divide that 'manifests itself when senior feminists insist that junior feminists be good daughters, [when] daughters are not allowed to invent new ways of thinking and doing feminism for themselves' (Elam, quoted in Baumgardner and Richards 2010: 224). An emphasis on individualism over collectivism is congruent with a vital stage in the process of self-determination, but it does not rescue Lady Bird from feeling herself to be incapable of making a grand Romantic gesture.

The centering of girlhood in third-wave feminism implied there was a corresponding teenage youth culture that aspired to join the underground feminist punk-and-politics movement associated with Riot Grrrls. As a youth culture, third-wave feminism was sex-positive, driven by music and aware that sex and gender were performative and could be ironised, weaponised too. Some feminists rejected girlishness as behaviour that played into patriarchal categorisations of women, but activist sections of this youth culture still reclaimed girlhood and femininity in the service of self-determination, using it to overturn victimisation and destabilise oppression. This youth culture engaged in what Kimberlé Crenshaw calls intersectionality, which is 'basically a lens, a prism, for seeing the way in which various forms of inequality often operate together and exacerbate each other,' although responses to this in the cause or guise of allyship can be performative too (Steinmetz 2020). Overlapping this third wave and occurring alongside postcolonialism and postmodernism, postfeminism engaged in tactics of creativity, performance, mimicry, pastiche, experimentation and subversion of the kind seen in the Spice Girls, where the exaggeration of individualised feminism under the banner of Girl Power could be startling but also superficial. Rosalind Gill's elaboration of postfeminism as a contradictory sensibility tallies with the in-betweenness of Lady Bird and includes the possibility of being different things simultaneously:

> Postfeminism is best understood as a distinctive sensibility, made up of a number of interrelated themes. These include the notion that femininity is a bodily property; the shift from objectification to subjectification; an emphasis upon self-surveillance, monitoring and self-discipline; a focus on individualism, choice and empowerment; the dominance of a makeover paradigm; and a resurgence of ideas about natural sexual difference.
>
> (2007: 147)

Gill's examination of the articulation of these ideas which occur simultaneously and can do so contradictorily is crucial to the self-determination of Lady Bird and the possibility of reading *Lady Bird* as a postfeminist text.

A Dispersed Clique

The evidence of Lady Bird's growing conscience and social consciousness is displayed on her bedroom wall collage, which features pioneer Riot Grrrl bands Bikini Kill and Sleater-Kinney; but beyond rock, punk and pop, which exhibit their own muddy mix of true youthful rebellion and manufactured mischief, one of Lady Bird's problems is a lack of contemporary role models. Put off by media culture's 'almost total evacuation of notions of politics or cultural influence' in relation to the pressures put on young women 'to make themselves feel good' (Gill 2007: 153), girls like Lady Bird are as likely to look outside the present to great women in history as they are to the eternally eight-year-old Lisa Simpson, for example, a misfit within her family and school with a kindred tendency to self-righteousness that corroborates her nonconformism. Belle in *Beauty and the Beast* (Trousdale and Wise, 1991) too: 'another poor, smart outsider in her late teens and a very, very big influence on girls who came of age in the 90s!' (Lester 2021). At heart, the members of Lady Bird's particular youth culture know that claiming and showing solidarity is their first grand Romantic gesture due, but their fragility and awkwardness postpone this out of fear that such gestures require means and talent, even genius. Thus, although they understand universality in principle and might welcome to 'their' youth culture (probably performatively, possibly problematically) the oppressed lesbian in *But I'm A Cheerleader* (Babbit, 1999) and the poor, gay, Black boy in *Moonlight* (Jenkins, 2016), they feel the need to figure out their own lives first, which might be part of the problem. Perhaps it would help Lady Bird to know there are more young women like her? But how with so few films and series about smart, low-income, young women could she and others like her know this before social media? This makes the biggest risk and spur to these young misfits to be thinking they are loners, for whom rare glimpses of similar teens in the unfocused backgrounds of television series about the heartthrobs and high achievers of high school such as *Beverly Hills, 90210* (Fox, 1990–2000) and *Dawson's Creek* (The WB, 1998–2003) only confirm what outsiders they are.

There is a clue to their dispersed clique in their dyed red, pink or purple hair, however, which Lady Bird shares with several other smart, low-income, young women in coming-of-age series and films such as Angela (Claire Danes) in the pilot episode of *My So-Called Life* (ABC, 1994–95), Maeve (Emma Mackey) in *Sex Education* (Netflix, 2019–), Elora (Devery Jacobs) in *Reservation Dogs* (FX, 2021–), Lola (Franka Potente) in *Run Lola Run* (Tykwer, 1998), Johanna (Beanie Feldstein) in *How to Build a Girl* (Giedroyc, 2019), Julie (Renate Reinsve) in *Verdens vertse menneske* (The Worst Person in the World) (Trier, 2021) in the moment she asserts her independence, transgender Jules (Hunter Schafer) in *Euphoria* (HBO, 2019–) and Mei Lee (Rosalie Chiang) in *Turning Red* (Shic, 2022), whose red hair comes with puberty and reveals her inner red panda. Dyeing is a performative gesture of self-determination that suggests indifference to popularity because it rejects stereotypical patriarchal ideas that associate youthful femininity with purity, while also reclaiming and exaggerating an aspect of girlhood (playing and experimenting with one's appearance and the feelings this provokes) that accords with the postfeminist vindication of girlishness evident in the Riot Grrrl movement. Red, pink and purple are all striking colours on the spectrum of the symbolic order. They push girlishness to an extreme without denying it, whereas green or blue, for example, can tip things over into outright rebellion as in the comic book and movie character identified with Margot Robbie, the schizophrenic Harley Quinn, who ties her bleached hair in two pigtails, one dyed red and the other blue. Playing with femininity with feminist intent, Lady Bird's red hair dye references the likes of the bright red bob of Riot Grrrl Niki Elliott of the underground band Huggy Bear:

SHELLY: You look like a bad ass girl in a band.
This makes Lady Bird feel pretty amazing.

It therefore references the reclamation by Riot Grrrls of the culture of girlhood, which is a period of intense vulnerability, because it is also one during which young women can arm themselves with red hair and feminist ideas in order to remodel adolescence as a period of power and emancipation. Unlike the sixteen-year-old Britney Spears in blonde pig-tails and make-up (who we now know was coerced into) playing into the male fantasy of the hyper-sexual schoolgirl in her 'Baby One More Time' video in 1998, the red, pink and purple hair of rebellious young women was 'transgressive because they were refusing a corporate view of womanhood' (Euse 2017). The semiotic burden of dying one's hair red can, however, present a challenge to the bearer who may be too young to shoulder the complexity of its symbolism and sustain the rebellious gesture, such as Angela in *My So-Called Life*, who ends up crying, curled up in bed beside her mother. Nevertheless, *Lady Bird* still manages to suggest that unlike the previous generations of young women who had burned things, built barricades and marched, Lady Bird knows that homogenised youth cultures have stopped initiating change. Thus she wonders if the time of the misfits is due.

Simultaneity

Lady Bird was released in 2017 at the peak of fourth-wave feminism, which arose largely because the Internet provided a new platform on which to disseminate information, unite resentment and organise dissent. Social media resulted in fresh energy and an immediacy that empowered the #MeToo and Time's Up movements. Online campaigns offered scope for allyship, demanded justice and challenged impunity, but they could also magnify discrepancies into discord, resulting in the denuding of the privilege and fragility of white feminism. In her defence, however, the Lady Bird of 2002 is still young, too late for the third wave, which ebbed away through individualism, and too soon for the fourth wave, which was pending the Internet. The youth culture that she inhabits is an in-between one and yet, as for the etymology of her name, those spaces are important. As the American feminist, queer, non-binary, transgender author Jude Ellison Sady Doyle wrote in *Vogue*:

> In the 1990s and 2000s, [feminists] were cast as the shrill, militant, man-hating mothers and grandmothers who got in the way of their daughters' sexual liberation. Now they're the dull, hidebound relics who are too timid to push for the real revolution. And of course, while young women have been telling their forebears to

> shut up and fade into the sunset, older women have been stereotyping and slamming younger activists as feather-headed, boy-crazy pseudo-feminists who squander their mothers' feminist gains by taking them for granted.
>
> (Doyle 2018)

So where to situate the 'feather-headed' Lady Bird in relation to feminism?

Because successive waves of feminism were dedicated to proclamations of women's rights, representing and rescuing women by opposing patriarchy, reclaiming femininity on its own terms and extending feminist principles to the similarly oppressed, the question of where to situate the character of Lady Bird in 2002 and her eponymous film *Lady Bird* in 2017 relies on correspondence between those two years and cognisance of what I shall call simultaneity. Simultaneity is awareness of successive generations being engaged in the same or similar or different but connected struggles and, as one generation changes, so too does the relevance and resonance of the previous ones and their impact on those to come, whose actions will be affected too. Simultaneity is what underpins Carolyn Steedman's *Landscape of A Good Woman*, a semi-autobiographical analysis of her own working-class girlhood in relation to that of her mother in which 'the past is re-used through the agency of social information, and that interpretation of it can only be made with what people know of a social world and their place within it' (2005: 5). Simultaneity is the reason why the metaphor of waves misnomers feminism because each grouping of protest into visible activism is not separate from any previous or following instance but conscious of its place in, and effect on, both. Simultaneity also incorporates Rita Felski's view that 'the recognition that "equality" is not synonymous with "sameness" could lead to an expanded notion of equality that can also represent difference' (2000: 130). In *Lady Bird* simultaneity is an awareness of an ongoing process of becoming in those present, even though to Lady Bird's mind her mother has stalled. It means that despite Lady Bird's plaintive question – 'What if this *is* the best version [of me]?' – she and her mother both gradually become aware that they are not the final versions of themselves. Instead, they are 'in a postmodern condition, where female difference has fragmented into multiple differences' (Felski 1997: 1). As with the genealogy of feminism therefore, their simultaneity develops to include awareness of these differences and of how changes in perception of their relevance to the present creates a fluctuating resonance that is tantamount to a shifting presence in the current moment, one that has consequences for the future.

To some extent, simultaneity resembles the concept of hauntology that Jacques Derrida introduced in *Specters of Marx* ([1993] 1994), which evokes the return of persistent elements from the past to the present as the ghosts of lost futures. In the series *Unorthodox* (Netflix, 2020), for example, where Brooklyn's Hasidic Jewish community reads contemporary racism as a legacy of the Holocaust, its co-creator Anna Winger sought to represent a 'doubling back on history' (Rosen Fink 2020), whereby the nineteen-year-old Esty (Shira Haas) escapes the confines of Brooklyn and flees to Berlin, which is the source of her community's trauma and yet the venue of her liberation. However, simultaneity also differs from Derrida by attending to lost futures that might be found in fresh activism or self-determination, thereby forming and informing a political consciousness as well as social and individual responsibility. Simultaneity provides a critical framework that bridges the supposedly different 'waves' of feminism and sets up new models of female consciousness that have the potential to realise allyship. Seeing the various 'waves' as not subject to a strictly linear timeline but simultaneously fluctuating in resonance, relevance and meaning means that the concerns of and about white feminism, for instance, must be understood in a fluid context. In 1984 Black American feminist Audre Lorde famously wrote that 'by and large within the women's movement today, white women focus upon their oppression as women and ignore differences of race, sexual preference, class and age. There is a pretence to a homogeneity of experience covered by the word *sisterhood* that does not in fact exist' (1984: 116). Following Lorde, perhaps, several reviews of *Lady Bird* by female writers in university newspapers and online magazines took issue with the whiteness of its feminism and made impassioned and important points (see Burton 2020, Potts 2017 and Kaul 2021), but they arguably missed the tensions between the year in which *Lady Bird* was released (since when their articles were written) and the year in which the film is set and its protagonist comes of age. A social consciousness does not manifest itself fully formed but depends upon experience to grow. Lorde herself attended parish schools and found her own voice through poetry, but it was not until she entered higher education aged twenty and spent a self-determining year at the National University of Mexico in 1954 followed by a degree from New York's public university Hunter College that her writing and activism ignited. Expecting or demanding that *Lady Bird* be a certain way in 2017 disregards simultaneity because it perceives changes from one fixed point only and neglects the contrapuntal one, which describes Lady Bird's engagement in a complex and imperfect process of becoming in 2002.

Lady Bird essays how a smart, white, low-income, young woman reacts to and reaches for what Jacques Lacan (2002) described as the symbolic order of the world with all its laws and conventions, competing and dominant ideologies, complex communications, intersubjectivities and complicated relations [see Figure 1.1]. *Lady Bird* thus explores how Lady Bird attempts to create new spaces for herself by means of various strategies and ploys of self-determination, while, in the gap of fifteen years between Lady Bird in 2002 and *Lady Bird* in 2017, Gerwig brings into focus the spaces between different iterations of feminism, correlative gaps between generations and distinctions between the time of a film's production and that of its setting. This all happens in relation to the central mother-daughter relationship, which is how and why *Lady Bird* accomplishes what Lucy Bolton calls for in her examination of the impact of feminist philosopher Luce Irigaray on the cinema, namely that 'the relationship between mother and daughter needs to be brought out of silence and into representation' (2015: 42). This is essential because 'for Irigaray this silence perpetuates the most atrocious and primitive fantasies that are an indication of an unanalysed hatred from which women suffer as a group culturally' (42–3). Consequently, *Lady Bird* not only gives voices and visibility to its mother-daughter relationship, but it also makes their dialogue and interaction resonate with other female voices too. Its semi-autobiographical ambition recalls that of the aforementioned Steedman, for example, who rejects 'the attribution

Figure 1.1 Lady Bird reaches for the symbolic order

of psychological simplicity to working-class people' (2005: 12) and claims a respectful space for:

> lives for which the central interpretative devices of the culture don't quite work. It has a childhood at its centre – my childhood, a personal past – and it is about the disruption of that [...] childhood by the one that my mother had lived out before me, and the stories she told me about it. Now, the narrative of both these childhoods can be elaborated by the marginal and secret stories that other working-class girls and women from a recent historical past have to tell.
>
> (5)

As shall be examined, other female voices that resonate in *Lady Bird* include that of the 20th-century mystic Simone Weil, who influences the aesthetic and ethos of the film, the Transcendentalist Margaret Fuller, whose manifesto foments a national awakening of American feminism, the writer Joan Didion, who guides the film's attention to time and place, and the singer-songwriter Alanis Morissette, who turns Lady Bird's inner voice into a yawp. All of these voices informed and surrounded Gerwig's education at the all-girls St Francis High School in Sacramento and her degree in English and philosophy from Barnard College, a private women's liberal arts college in New York, where Gerwig declares, 'I really found who I was' (Shaw 2018). These women are therefore allies in Lady Bird's attempt to escape a symbolic order that attributes what Steedman calls 'psychological simplicity' (2005: 12) to working-class women most of all. But how to overcome the objectification of women by other women first, which is something the daughter discerns in the mother's treatment of her and, in doing so, is guilty of too?

Two Female Subjects

The 'psychological simplicity' that underpins the objectification of women can be undone by foregrounding female subjectivity in various ways. On film these methods include direct address, voiceover and subjective camerawork and can involve the presence of autobiographical elements too; but authenticity in this matter remains the preserve of those female-centred coming-of-age films (most consistently, it must be said, in those directed by women) in which the point-of-view is weighted towards just one female subject. In *The Diary of a Teenage Girl* (Heller, 2015), for example, the worldview of Minnie (Bel Powley) is hermetic, sealed tight with voiceover and animated interludes allowing Minnie to make sense of what is happening to her in an affair with her mother's boyfriend. Foregrounding the subjectivity of a smart young woman can also validate the experiences and emotions of other characters, such as in *Gas Food Lodging* (Anders, 1992), where the voiceover of Shade (Fairuza Balk) authenticates the travails of both her sister (Ione Skye) and her mother (Brooke Adams) by being empathetic and generous, qualities which she extends to the male characters in a film about inter-generational female bonding too: 'He didn't leave her. And now, after all that has happened, it was the single gesture, the one true heart, which has already changed the paths of daughters not yet heard from, those not yet born.' Indeed, *Gas Food Lodging* achieves a benchmark authenticity in its rendition of a smart, low-income, white girl's point of view while extending formal empathy towards the subjectivity of the mother too, thereby approaching the simultaneity of mother and daughter subjectivities that resembles the representation sought by Irigaray and *Lady Bird*.

The matter of balance, symmetry and simultaneity in *Lady Bird* is essential to Gerwig, who has admitted:

> For me, one person's coming-of-age is another person's letting go. I was just as interested in the letting go. [...] I don't see a ton of great mother-daughter movies. I feel that relationship is not represented as much as I think it should be. Often in movies, mothers are shown as monsters or angels. I just feel that that's not true. Most mothers are trying their best, sometimes getting it right and sometimes saying totally the wrong things. Often in coming-of-age movies, parents are played in a less complex way.
>
> (Cornish 2018)

The complexity Gerwig sought requires two female subjects – mother and daughter – but the challenge of realising this in the coming-of-age genre and a medium that has mostly been made and seen from the male point of view is exacerbated by *Lady Bird* being located along a very thin and sparsely dotted genealogy of female-centred, coming-of-age films about low-income, smart young women that focus on female relationships and the interaction of working class mothers and daughters. *Gilmore Girls* (The WB 2000–7) foregrounds a mother-daughter relationship that is more sisterly than parental and therein lies its particular conflict, while *Anywhere But Here* (Wang, 1999) resembles the inverse of *Lady Bird*, pitting the introverted Ann (Natalie Portman) against her flamboyant mother Adele (Susan Sarandon) in several similar scenes: the film begins with them arguing in a car until Adele pushes her daughter out, they visit open sale houses for fun, Ann escapes to an East Coast college and the film ends with their separation in an airport; but the basic genealogy on show lacks credibility. Thus, after *Gas Food Lodging*, the next kindred film is *Real Women Have Curves* (Cardoso, 2002), which features Ana (America Ferrera), a seventeen-year-old Latina in East Los Angeles, struggling to find a way to achieve her own scholarly aspirations beyond the traditional, limited, class-bound resignation of her domineering mother Carmen (Lupe Ontiveros).

In *Lady Bird*, *Gas Food Lodging* and *Real Women Have Curve*s, before they can see symmetry and simultaneity in each other, mothers and daughters must confront the symbolic order, which means, as Irigaray proposes, that they must recognise that it is 'the patriarchal world that has confined women to motherhood' (2007: 126). Doing so, Irigaray explains, will allow a mother-daughter relationship to progress due to the daughter seeing the mother as a sexual and desiring woman in her own right, because this enables the self-determining daughter to situate herself *alongside* her mother as she grows up and 'into' herself as sexual and desiring too (1981: 60–7). Such a defining relationship does not allow either woman to replicate or claim the subject-object relationship in either (or both) directions between them. Neither does it allow them to succumb to the role of object in a subject-object order where the subject is male. Instead, it enables two female subjects to exist together simultaneously in a discourse that escapes the patriarchal framework, which is a common antagonist that can persist for only so long in holding them both as objects. Having mother and daughter as two female subjects thus allows for their separation and autonomy 'while also resisting the psychoanalytic tendency to propose the relationship with the mother as the root of all dysfunction' (Irigaray 1987: 10). The task is complicated, however: Irigaray acknowledges that 'there are centuries of sociocultural values to be rethought, to be transformed. And that includes within oneself' (2007: 4). Consequently, she argues that women need to obtain a subjective status equivalent to that of men and gain recognition for their difference, even though this means 'the whole framework of their identity has to be constructed, or reconstructed'; for how else, she asks, 'are we to give girls the possibility of spirit or soul?' (41).

Reconstructing Souls

As a linguist, Irigaray offers suggestions for reconstructing souls that can be transposed to the grammar of filmmaking as a synthetic example of the 'means of culture in the form of language and images' (2007: 91). She suggests, for example, that women 'play with mirror phenomena [...] to minimize the chances of being projected into or devoured by the other' (43). Many female coming-of-age films include the trope of a young woman examining her body in a mirror and several subvert it. Camille (Lola Cretón) in *Un amour de jeunesse* (Goodbye First love) (Hansen-Løve, 2011) diverts her boyfriend's adoring gaze at her naked body to her reflection in a mirror so that she can see what he sees in her and claim it for her own pleasure and self-esteem. Danielle (Rachel Sennott) in *Shiva Baby* (Seligman, 2020) moves from introspection to critical appraisal and on to taking topless selfies for her older lover-client, while Selma (Zoé Adjani) in *Cigare au miel* (Honey Cigar) (Aïnouz, 2020) exchanges a full-length mirror that fails to explain her attractiveness to boys for a compact that she holds between her legs in order to study her vulva. Using a mirror to reclaim the gaze by replacing the male gaze with the proprietary female one at her own reflection can also be play with serious intent that, for example, spurs Minnie in *The Diary of a Teenage Girl* to claim the gaze when she stands naked in front of a mirror after having sex for the first time and tries and fails to detect change in her own body. A similar scene in *Somersault* (Shortland, 2004) has Heidi (Abbie Cornish) performing facial expressions in a mirror to see if any innocence and spontaneity is left in the behaviour she rehearses for adulthood. Both films are about teenage girls who seduce their mothers' boyfriends and yet these mirror scenes autonomise the self-determination of both characters from judgement by males while dismissing the Freudian cliché of usurping the maternal figure. Instead, they find an equivalence between the mothers and daughters that is ironically heightened by the coming of age of the teenagers and the final mother-daughter reconciliations of both films. The symmetry of mirroring and the simultaneity of the self and its reflection explains too the numerous mirror-like compositions of Lady Bird and her mother beginning with the film's first shot of them asleep facing each other on the motel bed [see Figure 1.2]. The symmetry continues with them side by side in the car, standing in profile in the thrift store, and in many of their arguments, where they are balanced, but without them noticing their similarities, not looking *at* each other, not paying attention.

In *Lady Bird* mother and daughter tend to resist their symmetry as shown in the colour-coded tug-of-war about the choice of prom dress in the thrift store. The scene is based on the symbolism *of* the symbolic order and is foreshadowed by two others: the first in the hospital where Marion gives a co-worker baby clothes and admits to not being able to 'resist' the sexism that upholds gendered colours for infants:

MARION: Oh Luis, this is for you! I got it for the baby, I couldn't resist it.
He pulls out a frilly pink dress for a toddler.

Figure 1.2 Opening shot: mother and daughter facing but not seeing each other

LUIS: She loves pink!
MARION: Well, it's really more for you and Andrea than it is for the baby, and I'm sorry I didn't have time to wrap it.
LUIS: No, it's perfect!

The second scene to foreshadow the choice of prom dress has mother and daughter searching endless racks for something Lady Bird can wear to a Thanksgiving dinner, whereupon Marion finds a vintage dress that, being vintage, connects with her own girlhood amongst thousands in the thrift store. The moment provides a glimpse of her and her daughter's simultaneity:

Marion sees something. Holds it up. It's a beautiful old fashioned looking dress. Marion has found the needle in the haystack.
LADY BIRD: Oh it's perfect!
MARION: Don't you love it!

A later scene in the thrift store has them searching for a prom dress, however, which underscores Lady Bird's coming of age and reveals how their relationship also expresses what Steedman calls 'the impossible contradiction of [a daughter] being both desired and a burden' by a working-class mother (2005: 17). The scene plays out in contrasting colours because Marion is associated with blue on account of her nursing scrubs and Lady Bird therefore identifies with pink because it is *not* blue (and references too the thrift-store prom dress made by Abby [Molly Ringwald] in *Pretty in Pink* [Deutch, 1986]). Most importantly, the scene emphasises their developing asymmetry because 'for Irigaray, in order for women to preserve their specific relational identity, their self-defined otherness and difference need to have social and symbolic representation' (Bolton 2015: 45). With this in mind, neither colour is socially gender-neutral: Lady Bird favours the pink colour of girlhood and uses it to differentiate herself from her mother, while Marion, who is subsumed within a dominant capitalist-patriarchal symbolic order that uniforms her in blue, inadvertently enacts a paradox by firstly supporting her daughter's 'pink' girlishness and, secondly, by expressing her residual fear that the dress might not enable or guarantee her daughter's survival in the 'blue' male symbolic order:

Lady Bird comes out again. The dress kind of fits her, It's bright pink and frilly. She looks happy:
LADY BIRD: I love it.
Smiles up at her Mom, looking for approval:
MARION (*considering*): Is it *too* pink?

Gerwig thereby uses colours as bait for a trap of sorts, showing the workings of social conventions and ingrained prejudices, but also subjecting her characters to an initially fractious semblance of simultaneity caused by this rupture in their symmetry. Before they can see and recognise simultaneity in each other, mother and daughter must escape the oppressive order and achieve subjective freedom. Only when the self-determining daughter sees the mother as a self-determining subject in her own right, and vice versa, will their relationship progress. Not until a later scene will the film confirm the absolute simultaneity of its two female subjects by seemingly ending as it began, with the mother driving her daughter to the airport and neither communicating until it is too late, and one is gone. Unwilling to resolve matters in a teary, farewell hug, Gerwig lets the absence of one of them unbalance the film, meaning Marion drives away with an empty seat next to her and the lack of symmetry indicates (too late) the simultaneity that had been there all along.

Symmetry and Balance

Another of Irigaray's suggestions: 'Between mother and daughter, interpose small handmade objects to make up for the losses of spatial identity, for intrusions into personal space' (2007: 43). These items have both purpose and symbolism in female-centred, coming-of-age films and tend towards domestic items like handmade clothes, hand-me-down jewellery and homemade dishes of the kind identified by Joan Didion as crucial to a female-oriented, alternative and unofficial intra-history of favoured tales and bequests in 'Where I Was From' ([2003] 2006). They can be heirlooms on the maternal side, such as the embroidered napkins handed down to Nina (Leslie Grace) by her grandmother in *In The Heights* (Chu, 2021), who tells her they are 'little details that show the world we are not invisible'. Or they can be a child's offerings like Minnie's drawings in *The Diary of a Teenage Girl*, illustrating how she feels to her mother. In *Lady Bird* the aforementioned dress has this function, with Marion shown altering it for her daughter, thereby turning it into a handmade object that might close the gap between them [see Figure 1.3]:

INT. LADY BIRD'S HOUSE. LATE AT NIGHT

Marion, still in her nurses uniform, sits at the sewing machine, tailoring the dress she and Lady Bird found. She finishes, and then hangs it up quietly in Lady Bird's room. Doesn't wake her up, simply watches her daughter sleep for a minute.

Irigaray also suggests that 'in verbal exchanges, create sentences in which I-woman talks to you-woman [because] the fact that this

Figure 1.3 Marion interposing the handmade object of a dress between herself and her daughter

language barely exists greatly restricts women's space for subjective freedom' (2007: 44). Such 'I-to-you' exchanges are emphasised in Gerwig's script by direct questions and the frequent italicisation of 'you' in scenes that deploy mirror-like compositions of mother and daughter facing off against each other too:

LADY BIRD (*quietly*): Didn't *you* ever go to sleep without putting all your clothes away perfectly? Like even *once*? And don't you wish your Mom hadn't gotten angry?

The mirroring of mother and daughter is ironic because although they fail to see themselves in each other, it reveals that they are both engaged in a complex process of simultaneous becoming. This is explicitly deconstructed when Lady Bird brings up the sensitive, threatening, transformative matter of sex on which they might be expected to bond and the conversation takes place with them both in profile facing the bathroom mirror [see Figure 1.4]:

MARION: OK, well let me get to the mirror, I gotta get going.
Lady Bird backs up, watches Marion put on makeup.

The mid-shot situates Marion between her daughter and the mirror and is held beyond the dialogue to show them not looking at each

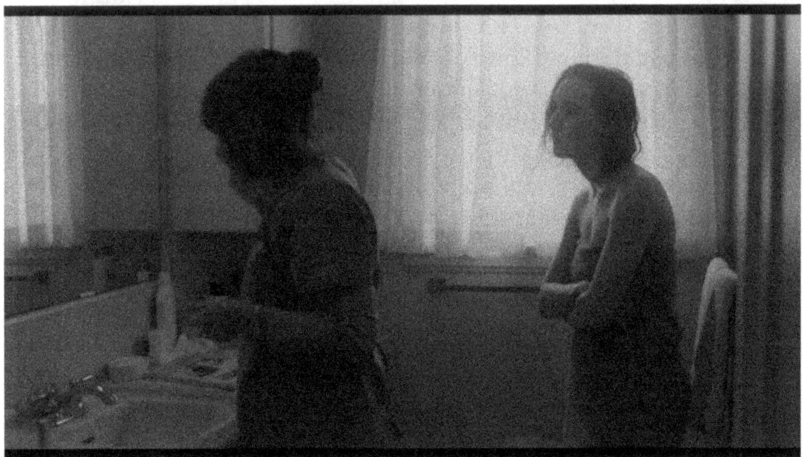

Figure 1.4 Mother and daughter regard themselves and each other in a mirror

other but paying attention to each other's reflections, noticing their distinct but simultaneous femaleness for the first time:

LADY BIRD: When do you think is a normal time to have sex?
MARION (*drops her mascara*): You're having sex?
LADY BIRD: No!
MARION: Uh, college is good, I think college. Use protection. Like we talked about.
LADY BIRD: Ok.
They regard each other.

The most effective of these scenes allowing simultaneous women to communicate is the one that realises a new symbolic order out of silence. Marion, who does not know why her daughter is upset, suggests they 'do our favourite Sunday activity' and, as the script states, '*Lady Bird nods, it would be nice.*' Mother and daughter then visit a house that is open for viewing before sale, posing as purchasers of a domestic space with potential to be recycled in the new symbolic order. In silence, mother and daughter wander through rooms and imagine what their lives might resemble, aware not only of each other but also, gradually and simultaneously, of the fact that both of them have dreams and, consequently, that both are changing. Any friction between them because of how they restrict the liberty of each other (by being born in Lady Bird's case and by not being able to afford her daughter's education in that of Marion) is temporarily suspended: '*It's a great day. Maybe the best in a long time. Maybe ever.*' In fulfilment of Irigaray, therefore, what this scene achieves is the depiction of 'women's rights to their own spiritual becoming' (2007: 88). In the silence of an unoccupied and available house, mother and daughter realise simultaneity and thereby initiate the self-determination that will follow because 'by destroying already coded forms, women rediscover their nature, their identity, and are able to find their forms, to blossom out in accordance with what they are' (Irigaray 2007: 103).

Cinemas of Girlhood

Lady Bird's attempts at expressing a subjectivity that can match that of her mother depend on her getting older and sometimes louder and being able to recognise the power of simultaneity by disregarding or 'unseeing' the limitations of the female role that she rejects for herself but identifies in Marion. The challenge to the mother, meanwhile, is to liberate her own longing, which, as John Berger diagnoses of the two subjects (mother and daughter) in *Landscape for a Good Woman*, is 'not sexual longing as such but the endless longing of the under-privileged that history (and life) be different from what it has been and what it still is' (Berger 2005). Instead of seeing only those limitations and lacks, mother and daughter must pay attention to each other as simultaneous women, not successive ones. *Lady Bird* lacks a scene in which Marion reflects on her difficulties conceiving, her resignation to childlessness and subsequent adoption of Miguel, but her hidden feelings at giving birth to her daughter are revealed in a shot of an unfinished letter to her daughter [see Figure 1.5]:

> When I got pregnant it was a miracle [...] and when <u>you</u> arrived I loved you without knowing you, I loved you when you were just barely an idea - when you arrived at 7pm (after twelve hours of labor), I <u>recognized</u> you - I knew that you were my girl.

This admission of recognition supports Bolton's assertion that 'women need a version of their own mirror so that they can become subjects and create their own space in the symbolic order' (2015: 32). Need is not the same as want, of course: *Lady Bird* begins with mother and daughter facing each other in peaceful symmetry but with their eyes closed, and then shows them side by side with their backs to the camera on the bed, before switching to them both facing front in the car.

Figure 1.5 One of Marion's many unsent letters reveals her true feelings about her daughter

Moreover, Lady Bird bailing out of the moving car is a performative gesture that exaggerates the independent and assertive phase of girlhood, one that she enacts during a heated argument to avoid seeing herself reflected in her mother.

A more germane mirror to hold up to the films of Gerwig is perhaps the cinema of Sofia Coppola, which Fiona Handyside defines as constituting 'a cinema of girlhood' because Coppola's films are 'concerned [...] with the position of girls and women within the privileged and affluent world of neoliberal postfeminist cultural norms' (2017: 12). The privilege and affluence may be alien to *Lady Bird* as well as to *Little Women* (Gerwig, 2019), but Gerwig's films do coincide with those of Coppola by showing 'the ways popular culture represents girls and girlhood through questions about postfeminism and its effects on the gendered organisation of present and future society' (5). Handyside's argument that Coppola's cinema is one of girlhood is (with one crucial caveat) applicable to that of Gerwig too:

> On the one hand, her films participate in postfeminist cultural norms (interested in femininity, questions of female agency and power, and showcasing friendship. Girliness, fashionable clothes and beautiful homes). On the other hand, they also draw on a significant feminist critical inheritance, showing her films as literally postfeminist (as in being able to learn from these interventions of feminist filmmakers from the 1970s, rather than disavowing them), and thus display a particular interest in questions of form that tend to be unusual in most female focused films.
>
> (13)

The caveat is that Gerwig's smart young women are low-income, lacking privilege beyond being white. The symbolic order that oppresses them, which Irigaray encourages them to reconstruct, is weighted, bounded and mined with economic restrictions. Thus, whereas the young, smart, white protagonists of Coppola's cinema of girlhood benefit from the fact that 'neoliberalism assumes that empowered individuals can exercise choice and agency to reach their goals, and takes no account of institutional constraints' (Handyside 2017: 3), Lady Bird and her low-income family, her unemployed father, overworked mother and menial labourer brother, are the victims of neoliberalism, denied choice and with limited agency, bombarded by institutional obstructions. Lady Bird and Jo March are nowhere near privilege or affluence compared to Charlotte (Scarlett Johansson) in *Lost in Translation* (Coppola, 2003), Marie Antoinette (Kirsten

Dunst) in *Marie Antoinette* (Coppola, 2006) and Cleo (Elle Fanning) in *Somewhere* (Coppola, 2010), who are 'trapped' in the Park Hyatt Tokyo hotel, the Palace of Versailles and Chateau Marmont, respectively. Consequently, the new symbolic order that Lady Bird must construct is one that is pragmatic and thrifty in order to support and potentially release her from those economic restrictions as an adult. This potential *beyond* girlhood makes it different from that glimpsed by the virginal suicides, Charlotte in the crowd, the guillotined Marie Antoinette, and the blasé members of *The Bling Ring* (Coppola, 2013), who although 'enabled by privilege' (5) remain in an 'eternally-extended girlhood that demands protagonists remain dutiful daughters' (36). Coppola's cinema of girlhood obliges young women to kill themselves while still virgins or be killed before the end of it like the last queen of France and thereby aligns any grand, self-determining gestures with 'the Romantic traditional approach toward agency (as talent or genius)' (17). In those of Gerwig, however, such gestures require self-determination, result in tiny triumphs over huge adversities and, in the absence of wealth and privilege, rely on loans, scrimping, support and the odd lucky break.

The Symbolic Order

The symbolic order for which Lady Bird reaches requires changes to the iconography and conventions of the female-centred coming-of-age film and the postfeminist youth culture it has attempted to represent since the end of the 20th century. *Lady Bird* makes its most revolutionary move by placing the mother-daughter relationship front and centre, but there are numerous other teen-movie tropes that it switches out in order to construct a new symbolic order for girlhood in relation to postfeminist youth culture in general and smart, low-income, young, white women in particular. Instead of splurging in boutiques like Cher (Alicia Silverstone) in *Clueless* (Heckerling, 1995) or hanging out in malls like Julie (Deborah Foreman) in *Valley Girl* (Coolidge, 1983), Lady Bird loiters alone outside a corner shop. Her first boyfriend is gay and, unlike the girls who wake and peek under the sheets at their 'freshly womanised' bodies in the likes of *Endless Love* (Feste, 2014), she is perfunctorily de-virginised: 'I was on top! Who the fuck is on top their first time!' She does not attract attention by dancing, singing, cheerleading or playing any sport or instrument well, and when Sister Sarah-Joan (Lois Smith) asks if 'math isn't something that you are terribly strong in?', she resignedly answers: 'That we know of *yet*.' She ends up in the chorus of her school musical and nowhere near to making the valedictorian address to her peers like Jessica (Anna Kendrick) in *Twilight* (Hardwicke, 2008) or Amy (Kaitlyn Dever) in *Booksmart* (Wilde, 2019). Most injurious to her victim status, she does not suffer the trope of the dead mother in female-centred teen movies.

In 2011 Kathleen Rowe Karlyn noted that 'sisterhood was the rallying cry of the second wave, and while representations of sisterhood or female friendship have begun to appear with more frequency in popular culture, the mother-daughter bond, a key model of female connection, remains invisible and unexplored' (2011: 8). In female-centred coming-of-age films, this is largely because the dead mother trope blights Andie in *Pretty in Pink*, Diane (Ione Skye) in *Say Anything* (Crowe, 1989), Cher in *Clueless*, Kat (Julia Stiles) in *10 Things I Hate About You* (Junger, 1999), Enid (Thora Birch) in *Ghost World* (Zwigoff, 2001), Lila (Gina Piersanti) in *It Felt Like Love* (Hittman, 2013), Cyd (Jessie Pinnick) in *Princess Cyd* (Cone, 2017), Sara (Julia Stiles) in *Save The Last Dance* (Carter, 2001) and Nina in *In The Heights*, to name just a few. This means that *Lady Bird* drops the sexist and simplistic Electra complex (which describes a girl's supposed psychosexual competition with her mother for possession of her father and idealises the union of the widowed father with his mothering daughter) and focuses on the mother-daughter mix instead.

But apart from an undead mother, Lady Bird's life lacks any semblance of uniqueness: she does not stand out like a midwestern white girl in an almost all-Black Chicago high school like Sara in *Save the Last Dance*, or Cady (Lindsay Lohan) in *Mean Girls* (Waters, 2004), relocated from the wilds of Africa to an Illinois high school, or Ruby (Emilia Jones) in *CODA* (Heder, 2021), the only hearing member of her family. Indeed, because Lady Bird's 'real-life drama' is not in any way special, her anguish is ripe for ridicule by her still living mother: 'Okay fine, yours is the worst life of all!' Lady Bird is less moneyed, academic and Romantic than Marianne (Daisy Edgar-Jones) and more like Connell (Paul Mescal), a smart, low-income, young man with a dead father and a yearning to write and study literature at university, in *Normal People* (BBC3/Hulu, 2020). She is not even treated to a tour of youth culture as it is divided into cafeteria cliques and schoolyard tribes in *Heathers* (Lehmann, 1989), *Clueless*, *10 Things I Hate About You*, *Mean Girls* and *Save the Last Dance*, mainly because Immaculate Heart is an all-girl Catholic high school in Sacramento, where the mostly white pupils all wear the same uniform (white polo, cardigan, pleated knee-length skirt, white socks). The only thing that sets Lady Bird apart is alienation from the religious elements of her education, which aligns her with but still separates her from other girls on the edges of their different religious associations, like Selma in *Cigare au miel*, who suffers the patriarchal rules of Berber culture, as well as Frances (Jennifer Grey) in *Dirty Dancing* (Ardolino, 1987) and Danielle in *Shiva Baby*, who negotiate Jewishness, and those growing up as Jehovah's Witnesses in *To verdener* (Worlds Apart) (Oplev, 2008) and *Apostasy* (Kokotajlo, 2017). In modelling a new symbolic order for a certain kind of young woman, Gerwig follows Irigaray in understanding that just because the maternal bond with a female child is not obeisantly ideal, this is no reason for the female genealogy to be omitted from patriarchal culture. Rejecting the social and cultural pressure for it to be hidden unless it conforms to 'systems of representation [that] are appropriate to men's subjectivity [and] reassuring to the between-men culture' (Irigaray 2007: 90), *Lady Bird* therefore recasts the female genealogy in ways that are informed by the simultaneity of becoming of daughter and mother too. The effect of this on Lady Bird's self-determination is that she begins to both separate herself from her mother and join her too, growing apart until she recognises that all women, including her mother, have the potential to do what Irigaray envisions and reconstruct their souls. *Lady Bird* may end with the physical separation of mother and daughter but its resolution is one of mutual emancipation and simultaneous reconciliation. Deciphering the new symbolic code of *Lady Bird* reveals that Gerwig's film is always and at heart a love story between two women.

Spiritual Becoming

Lady Bird's female genealogy suits the youth culture of smart young women because it insists on the rights of daughters like Lady Bird to assert 'their own spiritual becoming, a right in harmony with their sexed body instead of one that denies it in the name of an allegedly universal and neutral truth,' while at the same time insisting that mothers like Marion 'can't be reduced to motherhood' (Irigaray 2007: 88). The film even includes an explicit declaration of how Lady Bird commits to a process of self-determination that will allow her to realise her own potential, when she makes a performative gesture that literally enacts the process invented by the philosopher and semiotician Jacques Derrida for signifying his principle of *différance*, which is a neologism that combines the deferral of recognition of difference and the actual difference that this deferral will enable (see Derrida 1982). Derrida illustrates and enacts this philosophical process of becoming as one in which existing concepts must first be placed under erasure so that new ideas informing and issuing from a new symbolic order can be realised. Yet he does not erase the original concept entirely; instead, he follows the existentialist philosopher Martin Heidegger's process of discussing the concept of Being, whereby he writes the word 'BEING', then crosses it out, and then prints both the original word *and* its crossing-out. Doing so shows that the original concept is *sous rature* (under erasure, being inadequate but necessary for understanding of the process) and subject to dismissal pending the self-determination of the new concept (Sarup 1993: 33). Consequently, this new concept is subject to *différance* because, like Lady Bird's proficiency at math, the self-determination it promises is postponed and different from all 'that we know of *yet.*' Thus, in a sequence that follows Derrida, Lady Bird first writes her name (i.e. that of her 'being') on the audition list for the school musical in capitals as 'CHRISTINE "LADY BIRD" MCPHERSON.' She does not erase the old concept of Christine entirely but writes the new concept of becoming Lady Bird alongside it. Later, however, when the cast list is announced and she finds herself listed as 'Christine McPherson' in the chorus line, '*she takes the pen and crosses out Christine and writes LADY BIRD*' [see Figure 1.6]. Thus, she enacts a Derridean declaration of her potential to be self-determining in a new symbolic order that she is creating herself. In performing this Derridean conceit, Lady Bird subscribes to a process of self-determination that erases the notion that her generation is unable to initiate change because she throws the ball forward,

Figure 1.6 Lady Bird subscribes to a Derridean process of becoming

as it were, to be picked up in her future, as soon as she on behalf of her generation becomes able.

All these changes mean that instead of accepting history (and so her place and fate) as it is presented from the dominant position of the patriarchal order, *Lady Bird* and Lady Bird must favour and construct the (m)other's side. At the basic level of the coming-of-age genre and its representation of youth culture, this means that *Lady Bird* must oppose male authorship of stories about women and their frequent erasure of the mother in the dead mother trope. Consequently, instead of male authors like Shakespeare and Shaw dictating the behaviour of young women (*West Side Story* [Spielberg, 2021] is *Romeo and Juliet*; *10 Things I Hate About You* is *Taming of the Shrew*; *O* [Nelson, 2001] is *Othello*; *She's the Man* [Fickman, 2006] is *Twelfth Night* and *She's All That* [Iscove, 1999] is *Pygmalion* in a prom dress), *Lady Bird* shows the influence of Jane Austen on the female coming-of-age film (*Ruby in Paradise* [Nuñez, 1993] is *Northanger Abbey* and *Clueless* is *Emma*, while the older but no more together Bridget Jones is obsessed with *Pride and Prejudice*) and draws instead upon the influences of female writers such as Joan Didion and Louisa May Alcott, whose *Little Women* (1868) will be adapted by Gerwig for her second sole-directed film. Thus, on the (m)other's side of things, the female genealogy emerges and coheres.

Where Lady Bird Is from

Most impactful in terms of the genealogy of creative women leading to *Lady Bird* is what Gerwig has described as the 'spiritually seismic' example of an 'artist's eye looking at my home' that she found in Didion's writings on Sacramento (quoted in Dercksen 2018). To some extent, Didion has been considered more peripheral to Tom Wolfe and E.W. Johnson's concept of *The New Journalism* (1973) than male writers such as Wolfe himself and Truman Capote: their so-named anthology contains twenty-four essays and Didion's 'Some Dreamers of the Golden Dream' ([1966] 1973) is one of only two by female writers. Yet Didion's delineation of an alternative female genealogy for modern California in her own collection of essays entitled 'Where I Was From' implies a response to this example of what Irigaray has recognised as a system of representation that prioritises men's subjectivity and ignores a separate history of America and its women, of families and their women, of feminisms and all women. In response, Didion parses official histories and questions reputations in order to identify the male genealogy of California and its heroes as one marked by hypocrisies. Dismissing this, she then constructs a new female genealogy and symbolic order out of family legends of female fortitude:

> My great-great-great-great-great-grandmother Elizabeth Scott[, who] was born in 1766 [and] grew up on the Virginia and Carolina frontiers, [...] was remembered to have hidden in a cave with her children (there were said to have been born eleven, only eight of which got recorded) during Indian fighting, and to have been so strong a swimmer that she could ford a river in flood with an infant in her arms.
>
> ([2003] 2006: 953)

Instead of any written history, Didion recounts only what 'may be true or it may be, in local oral tradition inclined to stories that turn on decisive gestures, embroidery' ([2003] 2006: 953). Relying on the 'word of cousins' (ibid.), she constructs an elliptical, alternative history of America and resists the dismissal of such stories as hearsay by enacting Irigaray's aforementioned suggestion of 'interpos[ing] small handmade objects to make up for the losses of [...] identity' (2007: 43). Thus, Didion admits of an ancestor, 'I know nothing else about Elizabeth Scott Hardin, but I have her recipe for corn bread, and also for Indian relish' ([2003] 2006: 953), while also confessing that:

> [Of] my own great-great-great-grandmother, I have, besides her recipes, a piece of *appliqué* she made on the crossing [of Oregon]. This *appliqué*, green and red calico on a muslin field, hangs now in my dining room in New York and hung before that in the living room of a house I had on the Pacific Ocean.
>
> (953–4)

Finding truth in tales of female labour, endurance, stoicism, bravery and collaboration, in their details of girlhood and womanhood and a succession of mothers and daughters, Didion concludes 'Where I Was From' by recognising how the female genealogy she has unearthed resonates in her own life:

> You will have perhaps realised by now (a good deal earlier than I myself realised) that this book represents an exploration into my own confusions about the place and the way in which I grew up, confusions as much about America as about California,

> misapprehensions and misunderstandings so much a part of who I became that I can still to this day confront them obliquely.
>
> (962)

The act of writing down the stories of her female ancestors for the first time and verifying them by phenomenological evidence (such as the touch and sight of a hand-me-down *appliqué* and the taste and smell of corn bread made according to an inherited recipe) expunges Didion's disquiet about any mismatch of myth and reality and confirms her resolve to reject the male symbolic order and its patriarchal genealogy of America. As well as illustrating the strategy of Irigaray, Didion's labour also resembles that of Steedman, who states that 'personal interpretations of past time – the stories that people tell themselves in order to explain how they got to the place they currently inhabit – are often in deep and ambiguous conflict with the official interpretative devices of a culture' (2005: 6). To wit, Didion takes the (m)other's side of history and sets in play the means to self-determination for a new century that Gerwig, Lady Bird and *Lady Bird* attempt to follow through. A direct link to *Lady Bird* besides the film's epigraph is even suggested by Didion beginning her rewriting of American history by assuming the persona of the confused high school senior that she once was. Like Lady Bird, Didion recalls suspecting that there was something off about the male-dominated history of endeavour, enterprise and reward in the official books that she recited in her cliché-filled address to her peers:

> 'One hundred years ago, our great-great grandparents were pushing America's frontier westward to California.' So began the speech I wrote to deliver at my eighth grade graduation from the Arden School, outside Sacramento.
>
> ([2003] 2006: 961)

But now Didion writes of her remorse, having realised that this speech was a betrayal of her female ancestors and her peers, which could have been avoided if women had not been erased from history or she had done more to reinstate them.

Much like Didion, Lady Bird realises that acts of female self-determination can create 'declamatory breaks' with male-centred history in which 'we worry it, correct and revise it, try and fail to define our relationship to it and its relationship to the rest of the country' (Didion [2003] 2006: 975). Finding the official history insufficient and untrustworthy, Didion seeks out intra-history instead, that of the unwritten, interior, domestic space, which leads down through an alternative female genealogy to her perception of simultaneity and inheritance as a young woman in Sacramento: 'Our highest moment in this area was the acquisition, in 1951, of a house in Sacramento in which the curtain on the stairs had not been changed since 1907' (993). The image and her idea resonate in Steedman's writing too, when she reflects:

> It matters then, whether one reshapes past time, re-uses the ordinary exigencies and crises of all childhoods whilst looking down from the curtainless windows of a terraced house like my mother did, or sees at that moment the long view stretching away from the big house in some richer and more detailed landscape.
>
> (2005: 5)

Concluding her task of decentering the public, male genealogy and recentering the private, female one inspires Didion to identify links between capitalism, patriarchy and the military-industrial complex that resulted in the destruction of California, 'a state in which virtually every county was to one degree or another dependent on defense contracts' ([2003] 2006: 1038). This downturn began when 'General Motors closed its Van Nuys assembly plant in 1999 with 2600 jobs lost' (ibid.) and is still being felt three years later in *Lady Bird*, which rejects the male genealogy of most high school coming-of-age films (in production, themes, plot and protagonism), holding them to be injurious to the downturn that threatens and impedes the female genealogy that results in the particular youth culture that the film foregrounds.

Imaginary Wings

Finally, what leads into the prioritising of the mother-daughter relationship in *Lady Bird*, as well as the potential for self-determination of Lady Bird is Didion's warning about the consequences of foregrounding the female genealogy in her essay 'Notes from a Native Daughter' ([1965] 2006): 'Perhaps in retrospect this has been a story not about Sacramento at all, but about the things we lose and the promises we break as we grow older' ([1965] 2006: 141). Despite the coming-of-age genre pivoting on the younger woman, both mother and daughter grow older, lose things and break promises in *Lady Bird.* Marion even combines all three when she drives away from her daughter at the airport, while Lady Bird does the same when reaching for a space beyond the one between girlhood and adulthood, between the third and fourth waves of feminism, between the symbolic order of the official history based on a male genealogy of

America and the private female chronicle of self-determination that she has the potential to realise for a new century.

A myth in the making, Lady Bird is both birdlike and ladylike and duly defends the image on her campaign materials of a transgender Horus, son-become-daughter of Isis and Osiris, the god of brotherhood, now sisterhood, and the sky. Avian humanoids are common in folklore (harpies, for instance) and fiction (such as the Veela in *Harry Potter*) but they tend to have wings too. Being wingless, Lady Bird cannot fly away from home and school but she is working on other means such as loans and scholarships. As shall be explored in Chapter 2, education is both a means of escape and a means of entrapment in lifelong debt; yet the signposts of history all around her are unerring and she duly moves forward into higher education. Lady Bird is not, however, the culmination of a female genealogy and neither is she the origin of an alternative future, but she does exist in this in-between time in which historical, social, political, philosophical and literary influences lay out the choices made by others in her past and point her towards her own options for the future. In attempting to answer Irigaray by giving Lady Bird the possibility of spirit or soul, Gerwig subscribes to the 20th-century mystic Simone Weil, who contends that 'grace is the only exception [to] all the natural movements of the soul that are controlled by laws analogous to those of physical gravity' because whereas 'gravity makes things come down, wings make them rise' ([1947] 2002: 1, 4). The choice between gravity and grace depends upon the imagining of wings such as self-affection, self-reliance and self-respect on the way to self-determination. These imaginary wings are what liberate Lady Bird and her mother in ways that recognise how irony plays a part in their separation. Thus, the film ends by closing a narrative loop that sees Lady Bird eject herself from the car driven by her mother: a loop that began with a performance of teenage rebellion that results in a broken arm and ends with her being left at the airport as a result of her mother's performance of indifference, which hides the truth of Marion's dejection. This loop along with simultaneity and, as Steedman suggests, the reshaping of time, all derive from, and further fuel, the creation of a new and alternative female genealogy. It is this that adds irony to Lady Bird's attempts to separate herself from her mother, which Irigaray reveals is impossible because this bond is always there, only hidden beneath the weight of patriarchy. Even when her final phone call goes to an answering machine there is simultaneity: imaginary wings worn by both her *and* her mother in the moment that she calls her childhood home and finds that neither of them are there.

2 Class and Classes

Education and Consciousness

Lady Bird starts with mother and daughter crying at the ending of John Steinbeck's *The Grapes of Wrath* (1939), which tells of a poor family during the Great Depression, and ends on a resolution that prefigures Christine's assumption of a lifetime of student debt. As this chapter explores, the low-income factor in the youth culture of smart young women that *Lady Bird* represents brings to prominence themes of inequality, privilege and access in relation to how class, religion and education affect self-determination. It also examines the autobiographical elements of the film in relation to Gerwig, who graduated from her all-girl Catholic high school in Sacramento one year before Lady Bird in 2002, and the simultaneity of a film about Gerwig's girlhood being made by the adult that she would become. Assuming Lady Bird enrols in university in 2003 and completes a three-year degree, she will graduate in 2006, the year that the housing bubble began to leak due to ineffective underwriting of delinquent mortgage loans, a few months before the American and Chinese stock markets plummeted in February 2007. One year after she graduates, hedge funds will collapse, banks will stop dealing and federal funds will be withdrawn. The global financial crisis of 2007–08, which saw a steep decline in the repayment of student loans from low-income backgrounds, will mean that Lady Bird and many 'student borrowers who graduate or leave school during a recession might have trouble earning enough to repay their student debt, increasing the likelihood that their loan balances keep growing, or they default' (Blagg and Blom 2018). Defaulting on a student loan secured against her parents' property with a second sub-prime mortgage already attached will result in her case being handed over to a debt collecting agency that the government has empowered to impose high interest rates, pursue reimbursement, apply for court judgements, blacklist credit records for at least six years, and force debtors into sequestration, meaning the seizure of anything from its owner, including the eviction of her parents

DOI: 10.4324/9781003240907-3

from a home that will be sold for a marked down price at auction for the benefit of creditors. Then, Lady Bird and her parents will know the answer to the question her father asks a banker in 2003: 'So with her scholarships and then if we re-finance the house… Then where are we?'

Life before College

Adolescence is a manufactured space between childhood and adulthood, a period between natural, unmanageable puberty and an artificial, legal maturity that was invented when the modern age sought to eradicate child labour, indentured servitude and premature motherhood by inventing a space between stopping play and starting work. Not too long ago, this interval was impossible for all but the rich, whose life expectancy allowed for extended recreation and education. When post-World War Two social conditions allowed, however, even poorer, western families could afford for their children to fill the years twelve to eighteen with exploring vocations and so improve the community as well as their nation. Since the late 20th century, however, neoliberalism has sought to close that gap by erasing the years of juvenescence until even infants are fearful of how their grades will impact on their careers. Into the 21st century, moreover, and the shock and fallout of 9/11 and the ensuing trudge towards the calamity of the 2008 economic crash exacerbated the curtailment of lightheartedness.

Lady Bird's frustrations at not being able to afford to go to a college of her choosing are worsened, selfishly so on her part, by her father's unemployment, her mother's thrift and her university-educated brother's surrender to a low paying, unskilled job. The redundancy of Larry (Tracey Letts) also flips the notion of patriarch from one who is present when absent to someone who is absent when present, thereby raising the question of what happens to 'patriarchy in households where a father's position is not confirmed by the social world outside the front door' (Steedman 2005: 7). Does this 'fracture between social and domestic power' (73) create an opportunity for matriarchy or does the matriarch maintain a supporting role that is increasingly performative? Investment in Lady Bird's education suggests an all-in gambit that blocks the disappointment of her adopted brother Miguel (Jordan Rodrigues) working at a grocery store after graduating from Berkeley; but the pressure put on Lady Bird is building:

MARION: EVERYTHING we do is for you. EVERYTHING! You think I like driving that car around. Do you? You think I like working double shifts at the psych hospital?

The family's exhaustion is evident, moreover, in a political context marked by the failure of successive governments to improve the lives of those whose over-extended aspirations would be exploited in ways that would contribute to the economic crash. Numerous free trade agreements and, following the attack on the World Trade Center, a global war on terrorism that is focused on Iraq but played out along a new frontline of homeland defence, have brought economic depression to Sacramento. Indeed, 'according to the Commission on State Finance in Sacramento, which monitors federal spending and its impact on the state, some 800,000 jobs were lost in California between 1988 and 1993' (Didion [2003] 2006: 1041), meaning the Sacramento of *Lady Bird* in 2002–03 resembles that of 1973–75, when the OPEC oil embargo and Nixon's wage controls crashed the dollar and pushed unemployment to 9%.

Class misnomers economic stratification in America: 'I asked my mother to what "class" we belonged. "It's not a word we use," she said. "It's not the way we think"' (Didion [2003] 2006: 1037). But tensions do exist between horizontal lines of calculable affluence and the lack of it, which determine but can also be changed by education, while vertical fault-lines may divide the population even more on matters of race and gender. This figurative way of dividing things is treated literally in *Lady Bird* when Danny (Lucas Hedges) tells her mother that 'Lady Bird always says that she lives on the wrong side of the tracks but I always thought that that was like a metaphor. But there are *actual* train tracks.' The resulting grid creates pockets of youth cultures that struggle with communication and representation, which are exacerbated by terms like 'white working class' that undermine economic class solidarity between ethnic groups and imply the non-productive status of non-white populations, particularly when contrasted with the racial inference of categories like 'urban' or 'inner-city' youth cultures. Lady Bird, like Nadine (Hailee Stanfield) in *The Edge of Seventeen* and Vivian (Hadley Robinson) in *Moxie* (Poehler, 2021), is perhaps too young to realise that white feminism can lack intersectionality and be dismissive and ignorant, even toxic; but their understanding of allyship still has potential. In *Moxie* the acquisition of class consciousness, feminist engagement, allyship and activism suggests that Vivian's awareness of her own white saviourism is a trade-off with the effects of her school protest being occasioned by her privilege, while Lady Bird and Nadine defer their own activism to a point past high-school graduation as they currently feel like they have enough to contend with in respect of their own girlhood. Like Nadine berating herself in the bathroom mirror at a party – 'Just don't be so weird! God, why are you so awkward!?' – Lady Bird suffers a lack of courage, social skills and confidence as well as a surfeit of selfishness and self-consciousness stirred up by popular culture, advertising and the media, which can disrupt the link between self-determination and postfeminism.

In its portrayal of the pressures on young women, *Lady Bird* conflates themes of education, religion and autobiography by sending Lady Bird to Immaculate Heart of Mary, an all-girl Catholic high school where faith is embedded throughout the curriculum as it was in Gerwig's St. Francis High School in Sacramento. (And at this point I, like Carolyn Steedman, 'see my childhood as evidence that can be used' [2005: 104], and thus admit to and draw upon a Catholic education too, from St. Mary's Catholic Primary School to Mary Immaculate High School.) A Catholic school imposes a subset of rituals – prayer, mass, communion, confession – to maintain a behavioural code that emphasises self-control and self-censorship. (My teachers were mostly nuns returned from missions in Africa, now sitting missionless in classrooms.) Scenes at Immaculate Heart reflect the either-or exaggerations of schooldays, when there are good and bad teachers, boring subjects and fun ones, comedy (the football coach drafted in to manage the 'attacking formations' of the school musical) and tragedy (the priest whose method-acting exercise gives way to his emotional breakdown). But Catholicism is not the motive for Lady Bird's enrolment in a private Catholic high school; she is there because her parents preferred it to a public one, where violence is higher, teaching standards are lower, and pupil demographics are more complicated. (My Catholic schools were almost all-white and there was snobbery and racism in my parents' decision to enrol me.) But *Lady Bird* does not raise any ethnic or racial concerns about Sacramento, where the population is 23.9% Hispanic and Latino, 17% Asian and 10.9% Black (USCB 2021). Nevertheless, Gerwig's St. Francis was recently denounced by many of its own students and its Black Parents Association for condoning incidents of racism by white pupils (Sacramento Bee 2021). The school administration is blamed in a local news report (ABC 10 2020) and it duly responded with a Racial Reconciliation Plan promising 'a deep and reflective look at our policies and practices' (ABC 10 2021).

In *Lady Bird*, the only mention of race is in a family falling-out where Lady Bird suggests her adopted brother's grades were not the reason he was accepted into Berkeley:

MIGUEL: Meaning?
LADY BIRD: Nothing.
MIGUEL: (*turning red*) What are you implying. YOU FUCKING RACIST.

LADY BIRD: I didn't *say* anything.
MIGUEL: I DIDN'T PUT DOWN MY RACE!
LADY BIRD: I'm sure they had no idea, *MIGUEL*!

This points out the comparatively enclosed world of Lady Bird's Catholic high school and, consequently, the film. Few pupils appear to be played by extras of Black, Hispanic or Asian descent and the matter of allyship is not raised for Lady Bird, who is only beginning to suspect that her education is privileged and hermetic and, furthermore, that this is a problem. There are an estimated 51 million Catholics in the United States and the majority are of Hispanic and Latino, Irish and Italian descent, but films set in Catholic high schools tend to frame and ferment exclusively white male teenage angst in the likes of *Rudy* (Anspaugh, 1993), *The Basketball Diaries* (Kalvert, 1995), *The Dangerous Lives of Altar Boys* (Care, 2002), *Funeral Kings* (McManus and McManus, 2012) and *St. Vincent* (Melfi, 2014) or the criminal consequences of this repression in adult males in *Doubt* (Shanley, 2008) and *Spotlight* (McCarthy, 2015). Perhaps only the series *Derry Girls* (Channel 4, 2018–22), which is set in Northern Ireland in the early 1990s, and the Spanish film *Las niñas* (The Girls) (Palomero, 2020) can stand comparison with *Lady Bird* in essaying how hermetic are schooldays for Catholic girls.

Private Catholic high schools in the United States must abide by national non-discrimination policies, but Catholic families in California are statistically more likely to live in lower-income Hispanic and Latino communities like East L.A., where the median annual per capita income for 2015–19 was $16,901, half that ($32,751) in Sacramento (USCB 2021). This means that Catholic families are more likely to send their children to public, secular schools. Private Catholic schools tend to emphasise obedience to the institution, which starts with the uniform and continues via a support network of churches and community groups offering complementary extra-curricular activities. Uniform, ritual (mass, prayer), decorum and public duty are thus factored into Lady Bird's private schooling as it was for Gerwig: 'I'm not Catholic. I was not raised Catholic. […] I was raised Unitarian Universalist. But I did go to a Catholic high school' (quoted in Gross 2017). The current website of St. Francis in Sacramento, where tuition costs at present are $14,000 per year, duly boasts an alumna page for Gerwig:

> Greta Gerwig graduated from St. Francis Catholic High School in 2002. While at SF, Greta was part of the Dance program, Chamber Choir and numerous theatre productions. She played in

> SF's shows *Into the Woods*, *The Boy Friend*, *Pippin*, and *The Apple Tree*, as well as Lenaea [High School Theatre] Festival showings with SF for *Antigone*, *Final Dress Rehearsal* and *Ladies of the Tower*, for which she was a Lenaea medalist.
>
> (St. Francis 2021a)

This website also touts 'the all-girls advantage' for smart young women who would like to be 'Empowered. Nurtured. Transformed':

> Single-sex schools create a climate where girls can express themselves freely and frequently, and develop higher order thinking skills. Our safe and nurturing environment teaches girls to value themselves and their futures.
>
> (St. Francis 2021b)

Catholicism conflates the liturgical and academic year at St. Francis, where 'the Mass is the source and summit of our Christian life' (St. Francis 2021c) and the dress code for 'date dances' includes the edicts that 'dresses must be no more than three inches above the knees [and] girls may wear a strapless dress; however, no skin may be exposed on the stomach, back or chest [while] the male date for formal dances should wear a tuxedo or a suit and tie' (St. Francis 2021d). St. Francis is just one of 43,800 high schools (and 95,200 primary schools) managed by the Catholic church as part of the largest non-governmental school system in the world (Gardner, Lawton and Cairns 2005: 148). This all adds up to a global Catholic youth culture in which Lady Bird, like Gerwig, is only pretending to play a part. Richard Pring argues that the decision of whether or not to send a child to a private faith school 'hinges ultimately, not upon their academic achievement, the rights of parents, freedom of choice or a distinctive ethos, but upon the aims of education, the rationality of nurturing a particular set of faith based beliefs, the value of individual autonomy and the extent to which indoctrination should at all costs be avoided' (2005: 56). Avoidance of fees as well as indoctrination certainly contributed to the decision by the governing board of the San Domenico Catholic High School, 71 miles southwest of Sacramento in San Anselmo, to purge itself of Catholic rituals and paraphernalia when it converted to a state-funded public school in 2017 because 'not enough Catholics are willing to spend $42,825 for a year of high school' (Guernsey 2017). In the week that *Lady Bird* was released, the Catholic News Agency responded by stating that 'in order to appreciate how far San Domenico has strayed from its mission, it's important to understand the nature and goals of Catholic education. Catholic schools exist to help people get to heaven' (ibid.). Not college, heaven.

Catholicism

For a non-Catholic child in a Catholic school, good behaviour consists of following the faithful [see Figure 2.1]. Unless there is a family tradition to be upheld, this Catholic education will dehistoricise the child, making Lady Bird an experiment in social climbing that casts her as a hybrid creature like the Little Mermaid, zig-zagging between social classes like Cinderella, wanting a boyfriend with bookcases like Belle. Being judged by her learnt and rote performance makes Lady Bird see herself as object of exchange in a game of ownership played against the school and her mother, whose strategy is to demonstrate self-sacrifice and impose the payback of decent grades and decorum. She stands respectfully in line when '*everyone takes communion. Lady Bird approaches and crosses her arms so she just gets a blessing, not real communion, she's not Catholic.*' She even changes her name from Christine, which means follower of Christ, to that of the paganistic Lady Bird in subversion of the Catholic sacrament of confirmation. And she raises hell in a special assembly on abortion.

Abortion is, of course, one of the most emotive and complex topics in relation to feminism and self-determination. Sally Markowitz notes that 'one popular defense of abortion is based on the woman's right to

Figure 2.1 Lady Bird as a non-Catholic pupil in a Catholic school

autonomy and avoids the personhood issue [of the foetus] altogether' (1990: 1). This trade-off in self-determination reflects the emphasis on individualist feminism that diverged from historical campaigns for universal suffrage and sought to build on Roe v. Wade in 1973, which legalised abortion in all 50 states, with a range of campaigns for various civil rights. Roe v. Wade was overturned by a Supreme Court ruling in 2022 but abortion is still legal in California for those older than twelve and can be induced up to twenty-four weeks after the start of the last menstrual period or later if there is a risk to health. Indeed, the Public Policy Institute of California's statewide survey of October 2020 reported a 70% majority in favour of maintaining access to legal abortion practices, adding that 'across partisan groups, overwhelming majorities of Democrats (89%) and independents (77%) and a slim majority of Republicans (53%) do not want the ruling [in Roe v. Wade] overturned' (Baldassare et al. 2020). But faith-based demographics are different from political affiliations and Gerwig's St. Francis, which is the model for that in *Lady Bird*, is the only four-year, all-female, college preparatory, Catholic high school in Sacramento that is affiliated with the Catholic Diocese of Sacramento, which hails it as 'dedicated to serving young women and their families who seek a community of faith, excellence, leadership, and service, grounded in the teachings of Jesus Christ' (SCD 2021). This diocese promotes a pregnancy helpline 'so that women are better able to choose life for their pre-born children, rather than abortion. We also offer post-abortion healing to anyone who has been hurt by this very painful "choice"' (ibid.). It also recommends clinics offering advice on 'fertility awareness' as an alternative to artificial contraception that 'empowers women to monitor, evaluate, and care for their own bodies and reproductive health' (ibid.).

The 'special assembly' scene in *Lady Bird* features a visiting speaker called Casey (Bayne Gibby) offering kindly advice as an accompaniment to traumatising stories and imagery. (I recall an identical assembly at my mixed Catholic school that included a visiting speaker passing around laminated cards showing full-colour photographs of aborted foetuses before all the boys were sent away so that she could talk to the girls about abstinence and fertility awareness in preparation for marriage.) At a narrative level, the scene is about Lady Bird trying to impress her new best friend Jenna (Odeya Rush) with an attempt at a grand Romantic gesture that stumbles into activism and coincides with one of the most prominent campaigns in relation to feminism. On an even deeper level, Lady Bird's civil disobedience questions the role of aesthetics in moral philosophy and delivers a vivid illustration of Immanuel Kant's theory of judgement:

Laminated graphics about abortion are being passed around.
CASEY: That could have been me, that could have been my fate.
LADY BIRD (*to Jenna*) Just because something looks ugly doesn't mean that it is morally wrong.
Unfortunately this comment was loud enough for Casey to hear.
CASEY: What did you say, ma'am?
LADY BIRD: Nothing.
CASEY: Please share.
Lady Bird looks at Jenna and decides that she's really going to impress her:
LADY BIRD (*loud*) I said 'Just because something looks ugly doesn't mean that it is morally wrong.'
The girls are shocked and embarrassed, but laughing too.
CASEY: You think dead children aren't morally wrong?
LADY BIRD: No…
She's going all in:
LADY BIRD: I'm just saying that if you took up close pictures of my vagina while I was on my period it would be disturbing but it doesn't make it wrong.

By calling into question the limits of a reflective judgement of beauty that, as Kant states, 'reveals itself as a faculty that has its own special principle' (2000: 244), Lady Bird separates the aesthetic judgement from the moral one and denounces their conflation in the service of dogma. Kant's synthesis of empirical experience and reflective rationalism in pursuit of morality was the blueprint for Transcendentalism. Thus, when Lady Bird targets the subjectivist moral judgement of Casey, who demands that others share in her subjective judgement and frames this as a normative that allows her to 'demand such assent universally' (99), Gerwig is using Kant to get to Transcendentalism [see Figure 2.2]. As Lady Bird points out, linking aesthetic pleasure (e.g. at a picture of a baby) or displeasure (e.g. at a picture of an aborted foetus) with morality is a false equivalency because, as Kant states, there is 'no aesthetic judgment that could make a rightful claim to the assent of everyone' (98). Nevertheless, the doctrine that Casey propounds assumes authority and pretends this is a moral one, whereas Lady Bird follows Kant in questioning the universal validity of the aesthetic judgement on which this dogma is based. Crucially, moreover, she does this by reliance on

Figure 2.2 Lady Bird cites Kant and denounces dogma in a special assembly on abortion

the empirical evidence that is available to a young woman: the condition of her vulva during her period. In order to dissect the conflation of a belief that abortion is morally wrong from a reaction to purportedly gruesome pictures, she could have substituted 'up close pictures' of open-heart surgery, for example, and thus severed the link between aesthetic response and moral conclusion (i.e. the conclusion that open-heart surgery is morally wrong because it is equally bloody); but she presents the empirical evidence of her own vulva during menstruation instead. In doing so, Lady Bird demonstrates that her beliefs, which are essential to her self-determination, reject Catholic dogma and the imposition of subjectivist ideas of morality, particularly if they oppose her cognitive response to her own body. Second-wave feminists also rejected such oppressive tactics by conscious-raising exercises that included participants in women's groups examining their vulvas with mirrors in order to rescue them from invisibility and liberate female genitalia from pornography, which has tended to be a product of patriarchy.

Lady Bird's empirical evidence of the condition of her own vulva during menstruation inspires an opposing view to that of the Catholic Church, which celebrates bloodless virginity even after childbirth in the figure of the Virgin Mary and deploys this icon as an impossible ideal for young women. Her protest even overthrows the fact that 'the term [vagina] is hardly said out loud because of the shame and taboo attached to it' (Chakrabarty 2020), which explains the gasps from her fellow pupils, which rob Lady Bird of solidarity and any hope for collective protest. Instead, they prompt her to lose the high ground established by her Kantian critique of this attempt at indoctrination and she resorts to insults in her retort to the imposition of a moral value to non-evaluative cognitive judgements:

Sister Sarah Joan clocks Lady Bird's escalating mania. She briefly makes eye-contact with her. Lady Bird is ashamed, but uses her shame to plow ahead rather than turn back.

CASEY: (*horrified*) Excuse me? What did you say?

LADY BIRD: Listen, if your mother had had the abortion we wouldn't have to sit through this stupid assembly.

Her retort is faithful to the metaphysical context of Kant's critique because it posits a better world in which the assembly never takes place, but the insult still spoils the impact of her civil disobedience and prompts her suspension from school as the consequence of her integrity: her mother is furious, her father '*pretends to work on the computer*' and the subject of abortion, like that of racism, does not return. Yet this subscription to Kant links civil disobedience with feminist intent and remains current throughout the film, informing Lady Bird's oppositional, contradictory nature as well as her ambitions for meaning and freedom by means of self-determination.

Such 'special assemblies' are not exclusive to Catholic high schools: season three of *Sex Education* includes two, separate, gender-specific assemblies recommending abstinence and revealing homophobia in the secular Moordale high school. Yet the Catholic context of *Lady Bird* resonates with other films that essay the impact of Catholicism on contemporary working-class life even though films about Catholicism tend to essay male angst and rarely reference abortion. *Bad Lieutenant* (Ferrara, 1992), *Raining Stones* (Loach, 1993) and several films directed by Martin Scorsese, for example, focus on self-torturing males who struggle to reconcile the angel-whore divide in relation to the women in their tragic lives. Charlie (Harvey Keitel) in *Mean Streets* (Scorsese, 1973) claims 'you don't make up for your sins in church, you do it in the street, the rest is bullshit and you know it' and these films duly privilege the scourging of male flesh and punish women for impurity, such as Kay (Diane Keaton) in *The Godfather Part 2* (Coppola, 1974), who admits to an abortion and gets the door to the patriarchal Catholic system underpinning the mafia shut in her face.

In the coming-of-age genre, meanwhile, several films reveal a consensus on abortion as something to be endured alone and overcome together. Juno (Elliot Page) steps briefly into an abortion clinic in *Juno* (Reitman, 2007) but any moral element to her choice to leave it is fudged by a flippant series of flash cuts to fingernails (Juno having been informed by a protestor that her foetus has them). Otherwise, pregnant teenagers tend to be stoic, rational and supported by non-judgmental friends or siblings in films as varied as *Fast Times at Ridgemont High* (Heckerling, 1982), wherein Stacy (Jennifer Jason Leigh) emerges from the clinic to find her kindly brother waiting, *Never Rarely Sometimes Always* (Hittman, 2020), in which seventeen-year-old Autumn (Sidney Flanigan) visits a supposedly independent clinic offering advice and is shown a video to dissuade her, and *Sex Education* in which Maeve (Emma Mackey) undergoes the full clinical procedure and Ruby (Mimi Keene) takes the morning-after pill. In Northern Ireland, where until 2019 attempts to cause a miscarriage had been prohibited since the all-Ireland rulings of 1861 that reflected the Catholic Church's grip on the whole of Ireland before partition in 1920, *Derry Girls* treats abortion with similarly brusque pragmatism. Correlatively, the reference to abortion in *Lady Bird* does not foreshadow comedy or tragedy about the consequences of teenage sex. Lady Bird goes on to have 'unspecial sex' with Kyle (Timothée Chalamet) and this only prompts her to restate her protest about false equivalencies between aesthetic and moral judgement in criticism of his indifference:

LADY BIRD: (*fully angry now*) I was on top! Who the fuck is on top the first time!

KYLE: Do you have any awareness about how many civilians we've killed since invasion in Iraq started?

LADY BIRD: SHUT UP. SHUT UP. Different things can be sad. It's not all war.

Consequently, although Catholicism provides context in *Lady Bird*, it is a belief system of lesser relevance to Lady Bird than the Kantian philosophy that underpins Transcendentalism. The matter of abortion still serves, however, to spark an illustration of girlhood as 'the contradictory and categorically diffuse place between infancy and womanhood' (Steedman 2005: 127) in which beliefs and congruent behaviour must negotiate this in-between place and all its contradictions in order to realise a semblance of self-determination. Thus, the restrictions on her body *and* on her thinking make Lady Bird not only oppose Catholic teachings but also the way they are taught, dogmatically not Socratically. She submits to her high school education in Immaculate Heart as a means to an end, but her performance of faith is less than half-hearted. She scoffs unconsecrated wafers while discussing masturbation and pretends to pray while thinking about boys: '*Lady Bird watches the boys get communion. It's somehow sexy, opening their mouths to receive the wafer.*' For Lady Bird, who makes up her sins in church, it's all bullshit and she knows it.

Getting Out by Getting In

Lady Bird is an exception. Most smart, low-income, young women do not even apply to go to college, let alone the best universities they are qualified to attend. But in times of high unemployment, which is brought home to Lady Bird's family by Larry's redundancy and Miguel working in a grocery store, a university degree is still seen as both an advantage over others of her generation and a strategic deferral of entry into a hostile job market. Nevertheless, the low-income youth culture that she represents tends to demur from applying to colleges to the extent that there is only 'one high-achieving low-income student for every two high-achieving, high-income students' in the United States (Thorp and Goldstein 2018). Evidence suggests that 'affluent students get better counselling and more encouragement to apply to top schools, even when their scores are no different or even worse than their low-income peers' (ibid.). Bad counselling is notably offered to Lady Bird, who has decided that she has had enough of Catholic limitations on her self-determination:

GUIDANCE COUNSELOR: So I understand that you're not interested in any Catholic colleges?

LADY BIRD: No way. Sorry, but yes, no way.

GUIDANCE COUNSELOR: Then you'll be applying to UCs and State schools?

LADY BIRD: Yes, but also those East Coast liberal arts schools. Like Yale, but not Yale because I probably couldn't get in.

GUIDANCE COUNSELOR: (*laughs*) You definitely couldn't get in.

In addition, Lady Bird is late applying and all the interview slots have been taken by better prepared and wealthier students. Yet not being interviewed actually levels the field of applicants because, as the guidance counselor notes, 'it means that you'll have to get in on how you look on paper [and] your SAT scores are strangely very good.' The comment drips with prejudice that condemns the bias of the education system, which favours those who impress at interview with their clothes, bearing, accent and parents, for example, and finds high grades in standard assessment tests taken by a low-income pupil to be the aforementioned exception. What holds Lady Bird back is not her grades, nor her family's reliance on financial aid and loans, it is the lack of interest, expectations and support from schools such as hers for pupils from low-income families.

In order to combat this, since 2013 an application support package targeting low-income pupils with high SAT (Standard Assessment Test) scores has been sent out by the United States College Board, which administers the SATs. This innovation followed research into admissions strategies at Harvard, which found that even when:

> The [university] announced to much fanfare that it would officially be free for those with less than $40,000 in annual family income (now up to $65,000)[,] the number of incoming freshmen with family incomes below $40,000 was virtually flat, fewer than 90 in a class of 1,500, a tiny bump of only 15 or so students. Other elite institutions that had quickly matched Harvard's program reported even more depressing statistics.
>
> (Hass 2013)

In part, the problem with understanding this youth culture and the way its education is administered is that College Board knows who gets high grades but not which of those pupils is low-income. Profiling by area codes is racially problematic and asking students directly carries the obvious risk of that information being exaggerated, falsified or not given. Stanford economist Caroline Hoxby's response was to devise 'a complicated set of cross-references using block-by-block census tract data' that found:

> approximately 35,000 low-income kids with scores and grades in the top 10 percentile – and discovered that more than 80 percent of them didn't apply to a single selective institution. In fact, a huge proportion applied to only one college, generally a non-selective school that required only a high-school diploma or a GED, and where a typical student had below-average scores and grades.
>
> (Hass 2013)

Hoxby's solution was to design and send tailor-made information packs including costs, options and subsidised application strategies to high-grade students of low-income families as part of an Expanding

College Opportunities program. The result was that low-income students were

> 78 percent more likely to be admitted by a peer institution and 46 percent more likely to enrol in a peer institution. The intervention caused students to enrol in colleges with 26 percent greater instructional resources. [Projections suggested that] the program could yield a substantial payoff for students. For each $10 spent on the program, the interventions caused students to have college experiences that will likely translate into an extra $222,990 to $567,821 in higher lifetime earnings.
>
> (Hoxby 2013)

In 2002, there was no such interventionist support, however. Gerwig's own ideas about university at this time revolved around exploiting her talent at competitive fencing for a sports scholarship until 'it just became tremendously expensive, and then it became a thing of realising that it was such a financial burden, and I would have to have gotten a scholarship to go to college on it to make it worth the trade-off' (Gross 2017). In *Lady Bird*, Marion and Larry's social consciousness is hostage to a trade-off between self-sacrifice and huge debts gambled on the chance that their daughter and her degree will be worth it. Such inter-generational tensions inspire bickering from the start:

LADY BIRD: (*really picking a fight*) I don't even want to go to school in this state anyway, I hate California. I want to go to the East Coast.
MARION: Your Dad and I will barely be able to afford in-state tuition.
LADY BIRD: There are loans, scholarships!
MARION: Immaculate Heart is already a luxury.
LADY BIRD: Immaculate FART. You wanted that, not me.

And so *Lady Bird* suggests that in the United States with its all-encompassing free market system for goods and services, where education can be a commodity like any other, and where the failings of its public school system are the cause and consequence of poverty that leads to the cause and consequence of *more* poverty, only forceful acts of self-determination can make exceptions.

The Prodigal Daughter

Matters of authenticity trouble films about youth cultures but the labelling of these as semi-autobiographical can disperse criticism by means of the filmmaker taking responsibility for the psychological realism of a film. *Lady Bird* has much in common with *Les quatre cents coups* (The 400 Blows) (Truffaut, 1959) in and by which François Truffaut performs irrefutable auteurism by making a semi-autobiographical film about his own delinquent childhood. It also builds on *Girlfriends* (Weill, 1978), which Claudia Weill made piecemeal with small grants as a film about a would-be photographer who gets by on commissions, and *Smithereens* (Seidelman, 1982), made when Susan Seidelman was a recent graduate from New York University's Tisch School of the Arts and still part of the post-punk scene that the film depicts. Gerwig has maintained an uneasy balance between the veracity of her film – 'I really wanted to make a movie that was a reflection on home [that] has a core of truth that resonates with what I know' – and her dismissal of its autobiographical elements: 'Nothing in the movie literally happened in my life' (quoted in Erbland 2017). Yet Gerwig was born in 1983 in Sacramento and attended the Catholic all-girl St. Francis High School as a non-Catholic pupil. Her mother was a nurse. Her father was a computer programmer. After graduating, she left Sacramento to study English and Philosophy at Barnard, an East Coast college. She describes herself as 'the opposite of Lady Bird' (Cornish 2018) but:

> She has, she says, always been subject to fierce passions and obsessions. 'I was an intense child. When I loved an activity, I had trouble doing it halfway. It was scary with ballet – I would have gone to class for four hours a day, seven days a week, if I could have. And it's kind of a cultish world. [My teacher] gave everybody "ballet names", which put my mum over the edge: "She gave you another name?!"' What was it? 'My ballet name was supposed to be Scarlett, and my mum was like, "No, she can call you by your given name, this is a cult." She freaked out.'
>
> (Brockes 2013)

So where does one intense young woman with a given name and a mother prone to over-reacting end and the other one take over? With leaving Sacramento?

Gerwig had planned to study musical theatre at New York's Columbia University:

> And I liked it. But when I went to Barnard [College], I wanted to be all the women I met there. I was instantly drawn to the place and the women. They all seemed like superheroes to me. [I] was wide-eyed exploring the city [and] the process of learning it as my

> home was so fundamentally exciting. That's how I really learned about movies. I can't express enough gratitude for my time at Barnard.
>
> (quoted in Shaw 2018)

She took part in The Varsity Show, improvisational comedy, and hung out in the Museum of the Moving Image in Queens and the Film Forum in Greenwich Village, falling in with the Mumblecore crowd: a group of collaborative, multi-tasking, low-to-no-budget filmmakers that included Joe Swanberg, who gave Gerwig her first role in the largely improvised *LOL* (Swanberg, 2006), and Jay and Mark Duplass, who tagged her for the meta-horror *Baghead* (Duplass and Duplass, 2008). Gerwig also co-wrote and starred in *Hannah Takes the Stairs* (Swanberg, 2007) as a directionless postgraduate with too many life and love choices, before co-writing, co-directing and co-starring in *Nights and Weekends* (Gerwig and Swanberg, 2008), which essayed a long-distance relationship with two sides to its telling. Her breakthrough roles were in *Greenberg* (Baumbach, 2010) and *Damsels in Distress* (Stillman, 2011). Her co-writing of *Frances Ha* (Baumbach, 2012) and *Mistress America* (Baumbach, 2015), in both of which she starred, led to a succession of memorable character parts in *Maggie's Plan* (Miller, 2015), *Wiener-Dog* (Solondz, 2016), *Jackie* (Larraín, 2016), *20th Century Women* (Mills, 2016), *Isle of Dogs* (Anderson, 2018), *White Noise* (Baumbach, 2022) and a recurring role in *The Mindy Project* (Fox, 2012–15; Hulu, 2015–17). Janet Harbord observes that Gerwig has an 'emphatically gestural style of performance [that delivers] incomplete and imperfect performances of heterosexual femininity' (2019: 177–9) and this performative aspect of girlhood is threaded through Gerwig's script for *Lady Bird.* As Lady Bird, Saoirse Ronan is more contained in her anxious energy, working up to gestures rather than trying to rein them in like Gerwig. Gerwig's reliance on Ronan to lead her first two films as sole director therefore suggests a strategy by which Gerwig 'steps aside as an actor yet consolidates her star persona through the singularity of her focus on questions of what it means to accede from girlhood to womanhood' (184).

From Sacramento schoolgirl to Oscar nominee in just fifteen years suggests the kind of role model that Lady Bird was lacking. It also highlights, however, what Steedman has diagnosed as 'the difficulty of linking past and present in writing about working-class life, and the result of this difficulty in novels that either show the past to be a regional zone of experience in which the narrator cancels her present from the situation she is describing, or which are solely about the experience of flight' (2005: 20). In a sense, *Lady Bird* has its prophecy of self-determination fulfilled by the person who directed it, though Gerwig's denial of autobiographical links between herself and Lady Bird also allows the story of Lady Bird to work towards promise and uncertainty simultaneously because:

> The kind of cancellation of a writer's present from the past may take place because [...] stories work by a process of temporal revelation: they move forward in time in order to demonstrate a state of affairs. The novel that works in this way employs contingency, that is, it works towards the revelation of something not quite certain, but *there*, nevertheless, waiting to be shown by the story, and the story gets told without revealing the shaping force of the writer's current situation.
>
> (Steedman 2005: 20)

Simultaneity is there in Gerwig maturing as a filmmaker by making a film about the coming of age of a girl whose experience is partly based on her own adolescence. Indeed, as noted, the scene in which Lady Bird tampers with the cast list of her high-school musical reveals a Derridean manoeuvre that also applies to Gerwig crossing her real self out and then writing her screenplay for *Lady Bird* alongside her own crossed-out but visible youth. Raymond Williams holds that this process is essential to writers 'who had grown up inside a working-class community and sought to create its world - typically the world of childhood or of the family, while cancelling their present selves from this original situation' (2015: 271–2). He asserts that 'their theme was really escape from the working class - the experience of flight' (272), which suggests that Lady Bird's flight can be read as a betrayal of her class. Escape might be edifying for her but debilitating for the family and community she leaves behind – at least until she might return as the prodigal daughter: a filmmaker perhaps, who makes a film about growing-up in Sacramento. Such creative tensions are clarified by Williams' illumination of their prominence in his own novels about young persons' flight:

> They lacked any sense of the continuity of working-class life, which does not cease just because one individual moves out of it, but which also itself changes internally. Often these novels would display very rude attitudes towards the world where they were arriving, and sometimes sentimental recollections of the world which they were leaving. But they were not about what interested

> me most, which was a continuing tension, with very complicated emotions and relationships running through it, between two different worlds that needed to be rejoined. There was no form for this. I found that what I was writing was an experience of uncertainty and contradiction, which was duplicated in the problem of discovering a form for it.
>
> (ibid.)

Thus *Lady Bird*, which is all about overcoming uncertainties and contradictions, exhibits tensions caused by an older Gerwig rejoining the world and class of her girlhood and finding a form for its telling that is a teenage girl with a given name alongside her own crossed-out self as a teenager.

The Continuity of Working-Class Life

There are no sequels to any of the female-centred coming-of-age films mentioned in this book besides *Save the Last Dance 2: Stepping Up* (Petrarca, 2006), which uses the title but none of the original cast. Only a deleted scene entitled 'One Year later' on the region 1 DVD of *Real Women Have Curves* contends with the continuity of working-class life after leaving school and home. This unique 'mini-sequel' follows a film about Mexican-American Ana leaving her mother and the Latino community of East L.A. for an East Coast college. Ostensibly similar to *Lady Bird*, *Real Women Have Curves* is different because Ana's class consciousness is rooted in her cultural identity and its pre-immigration roots, while Lady Bird exhibits a false consciousness based on her personalised competitiveness with those of her own class and culture in Sacramento. Consequently, the deleted scene has Ana return from Columbia University in New York to her Mexican-American community in East L.A. and reconcile with her mother, who, like Marion in *Lady Bird*, had stubbornly refused to see off her daughter at the airport. Unlike the white working-class of Sacramento to which Lady Bird belongs, which defines class on economic grounds, the continuity of working-class life in East L.A. is racially specific: the welcome afforded Ana shows that her going to college is inspirational for her Mexican-American community and similar to what Nina going to Stanford means for the Latino community of *In the Heights*. Statistics that contextualise these distinctions reveal that East L.A. is 96.2% Hispanic and Latino (more than any other urban centre in the United States) and yet only 52.3% of these inhabitants are high school graduates, while Sacramento is 62.8% white and boasts 87.7%

of its population with high school diplomas (USCB 2021). Alongside Ana, Lady Bird is comparatively unoppressed and relatively ignorant of her privilege. Only 8.7% of the population of East L.A. has a bachelor's degree, whereas in Sacramento that almost quadruples to 30.9% (ibid.). Ana has less than a 1 in 10 chance of flight, while for Lady Bird it is 1 in 3.

Although Lady Bird and Ana share the same ambition of studying at an East Coast college, Ana's is on behalf of her family, community and class, while Lady Bird's is inherently competitive and reaches beyond the family and friends that she thinks weighs her down. Despite Ana gaining a grant, her parents think universities are only for successive generations of wealthy, white students (which is corroborated by Nina's experience of racism at Stanford in *In the Heights*), while Lady Bird's parents see their daughter going to college as her right and are prepared to mortgage all they have to maintain it. While Ana returns, however, and working-class life continues, Lady Bird sees her social order as transactional and tries to bargain up, distancing herself from her family and friends by pretending she lives in a different house and ditching Julie (Beanie Feldstein) for Jenna. Thus, the ambitious Lady Bird is repeatedly accused of being selfish. Her own mother tells her 'you don't care about anyone but yourself' and Julie agrees: '[You] can't do anything unless you're the center of attention, can you?' Her selfishness is not yet permanent, however, and mostly due to what Steedman calls 'a desire to be part of a story, even if it is someone else's' (2005: 77). Accordingly, Lady Bird's ambitions are so consuming that she imagines her future as a fiction of class betrayal and murder:

LADY BIRD: If Danny and I get married and then his grandma died, I'd inherit the dream house.
JULIE: Wouldn't his parents get it?
LADY BIRD: Oh yeah, we'd have to kill them. And we'd have to kill his older brothers too.

With each fiction and transaction, Lady Bird gets further away from class consciousness, negotiating her way to a version of herself in which the performative element fits with her plans for self-determination. Her class consciousness only begins to flicker when the problems arising from her wanting to flee are linked by her parents to wider concerns of social hardship:

LADY BIRD: Are you and Mom gonna get a divorce over this?
LARRY: No. We can't afford to.

Marion tries to avoid her daughter's ire, teach her some virtue, and assuage her own disappointment with life too:

MARION: Money is not life's report card. Being successful doesn't mean anything in and of itself. It just means that you're successful. But that doesn't mean that you're happy.

But Lady Bird's immature attempts at self-determination still jar with her mother's practical objections:

MARION: We don't need to buy that.
LADY BIRD: It's only three dollars. I'm having a hard week.
MARION: Well, if you wanna read it, we can go down to the public library.
LADY BIRD: I wanna read it in bed.
MARION: That's something that rich people do. We're not rich people.

Despite such solipsism, *Lady Bird* suggests that a potential for class consciousness can overcome a false consciousness and that education is a way to transgress the social stratification maintained by the sedimentation of wealth. It also points to the origins of the student loan crisis that saw the amount of student debt more than triple from $500 billion in Lady Bird's graduation year of 2006 to $1.76 trillion in 2022, causing fractious debate over loan forgiveness to blite the presidency of Joe Biden (Aratani 2022). Unlike coming-of-age films that deploy the trope of a scholarship like a magic wand, moreover, *Lady Bird* acknowledges the debts that those who head for college both leave behind with their families and defer till after their graduation, which totals 43.4 million Americans with outstanding student loans amounting to $1.6 trillion in 2022. (Hanson 2022). It suggests too that the degrees earned by Miguel, who works on a checkout, and Larry, unemployable at fifty-six, do not guarantee employment and only increase indenture to banks that offer student loans as a lead-in to first and second mortgages, further loans, and expensive, tied-in, long-term insurance policies. Thus, it points to the consequences of abandoning one's social class to gamble on higher education and it warns that doing so can cement frustration and foster resentment at what seems like privilege, especially for those women who participate on the basis of loans and make up 25.3 million of the indebted student borrowers as opposed to only 18.1 million of men (ibid.).

The question of whether this relative privilege of Lady Bird can warrant and sustain a drama is posed by Steedman, who remarks that 'the problem with most childhoods lived out in households maintained by social class [...] is that they simply are not bad enough to be worthy of attention' (2005: 9). But, as Steedman also notes, this is only because 'class-consciousness has not been conceived of as psychological consciousness' (13). Gerwig's script for *Lady Bird* aligns with Steedman's writing about her girlhood, being subject to 'a particular set of emotional and psychological circumstances [that] ensured that at the time, and for many years after it was over and I had escaped, [that] I thought of it as ordinary, a period of relative material ease, just like everybody else's childhood' (9, 13). Gerwig seems to agree with Steedman's realisation that the circumstances of their low-income childhoods are gendered, moreover, and that 'the attribution of psychological sameness to the figures in the working-class landscape has been made by men' (14). The fact that Steedman and Gerwig rescue their semi-autobiographical, smart, white, low-income female characters from being assessed on what Didion in her essay 'On Self-Respect' calls their 'passive virtues' ([1961] 2006: 109) is a challenge to such attribution, which informs a common trope in coming-of-age films in which young white females look past prom towards fulfilment by acceptance for further study in the likes of Juilliard in *Save the Last Dance*, Sarah Lawrence in *10 Things I Hate about You* and Berklee in *CODA*. This is problematic because it compartmentalises white female ambition in liberal, creative and performing arts, whereas the degree subjects of Hispanics like Ana in *Real Women Have Curves* and Nina in *In the Heights* are not named but implicitly business-like, leaving Vanessa (Melissa Barrera) in *In The Heights* to further her ambitions in the creative art of fashion design by scavenging for scraps of material in dumpsters. Meanwhile, Black females like Monica (Sanaa Lathan) in *Love and Basketball* (Prince-Bythewood, 2000) tend to depend on being recruited by a college team and even then are outliers to Black males off to college on scholarships like Ray (Jay Reeves) in *Safety* (Hudlin, 2020) and Michael (Quinton Aaron) in *The Blind Side* (Hancock, 2009) amongst others. When Lady Bird comes up from the New York subway she is at West 4th Street, New York University is a two-minute stroll away and the Angelika Film Center and the SoHo Playhouse are both nearby offering opportunities familiar to Gerwig. Yet when she is unpacking in her dorm room she discovers an envelope put there by her father, unfinished letters from her mother fall out, and the impact of her exile from her working-class community, in all senses, hits home.

Contrapuntal Simultaneity

The aforementioned cultural theorist Raymond Williams was writing about Welsh writers who left Wales and their working-class communities to study elsewhere, when he stated:

> Writers who stayed in the working-class had great difficulties with the novel as such, tending to move towards the autobiography [...] while those who moved out of it [...] produced novels of an enclosed working-class world in which the movement outwards was not part of the fiction - people have to get away for economic reasons, but the experience of combined continuity and discontinuity didn't enter as a theme.
>
> (2015: 273)

In his own writing, Williams attempts contrapuntal subjectivity, seeing the enclosed working-class world both from within and beyond it. His creative and critical framework resembles Edward Saïd's elaboration of the contrapuntal perspective of the exile and it chimes with the idea of simultaneity too:

> Most people are principally aware of one culture, one setting, one home; exiles are aware of at least two, and this plurality of vision gives rise to an awareness of simultaneous dimensions, an awareness that – to borrow a phrase from music – is contrapuntal.
>
> (Saïd 2001: 186)

By combining Williams and Saïd with the notion of simultaneity, a critical framework for the study of *Lady Bird* and similar films with semi-autobiographical elements about childhood and adolescence coheres. What I call contrapuntal simultaneity in relation to these elements in *Lady Bird* means that the distance between the actual events and their recreation on film is traversed in both directions, following Gerwig's adult memory backwards to her youth and tracing Lady Bird's youthful ambition forwards to the filmmaker. The same could be said of *Les quatres cents coups* and many semi-autobiographical films such as *Cinema Paradiso* (Tornatore, 1988), *Roma* (Cuarón, 2018) and *È stata la mano di Dio* (The Hand of God) (Sorrentino, 2021) by which male filmmakers claim incontrovertible auteurism by making films about their youth, in which the distance between childhood and adulthood denotes exile from youth because the author-filmmaker is one 'for whom habits of life, expression or activity in the new environment inevitably occur against the memory of these things in another environment' (Saïd 2001: 186). Differently and more uniquely, however, *Lady Bird* is a semi-autobiographical, coming-of-age film made by a female writer-director. Contrapuntal simultaneity is achieved because Gerwig's journey back to her schooldays in Sacramento is a journey forward in the career of a comparatively rare female filmmaker too. Indeed, the journeys are simultaneous because the self-determination attempted by Lady Bird corresponds with that of Gerwig in making a film that corroborates how 'class and gender, and their articulations, are the bits and pieces from which psychological selfhood is made' (Steedman 2005: 7). To borrow from Saïd, 'there is a unique pleasure in this sort of apprehension' (2001: 186), which is evoked by the combined travails of Lady Bird and the achievements of the film that contains her. This prompts us to read Gerwig's emergence as a filmmaker alongside Lady Bird's emergence as a young adult in terms of how 'women may learn the official dimensions of class-consciousness by virtue of their entry into the labour market and by adopting forms of struggle and understanding evolved by men' (Steedman 2005: 13). So what were the obstacles that would have faced Lady Bird upon graduating in 2006 if she were to become a filmmaker like Gerwig in 2017?

Lady Bird leaves behind a lack of liberty in Sacramento for the privilege of a liberal arts education in New York; but if, like Gerwig, she then decides she wants to act, write and direct films in the next fifteen years, she will have to deal with the kind of inequality detailed by the Annenberg Inclusion Initiative: only 31.8% of speaking characters were girls or women in the films of 2017, only 4.3% of directors were female and 83.7% of those were statistically unlikely to make more than one film (Annenberg 2020). Furthermore, there were only 43 unique female directors between 2007 and 2017 and only seven of those were from an underrepresented racial or ethnic group. Of the top 100 films of 2017 only eight were directed by women, including *Lady Bird*, which was released at a time when revelations about inequality, harassment and sexual misconduct, particularly in the film and television industries, were shifting from statistics to testimonies from victims, and from generalisations to accusations of individuals. This context underlines the uniqueness of *Lady Bird* as a coming-of-age film with two female leads that was written and directed by an actor and writer whose transition to directing was its own act of self-determination, one that would lead to a second and third film about female emancipation, *Little Women* and *Barbie* (2023). As Gerwig has acknowledged, her success as an individual comes with responsibility for others:

> I and other women, [we] feel that this moment has been a long time in coming and we're also feeling terrified that we're going to now say the wrong thing. The thing that I keep coming back to is, for me as a woman, particularly young women who have

> dreams of being part of this industry and this space of artists and dream-makers, and how protected that space should be.
>
> (quoted in Gross 2017)

Gerwig's concern for the safety of young women entering the film industry sheds an interesting light on *Lady Bird* and confirms contrapuntal simultaneity because, while her script posits getting out of Sacramento as a vital ambition, her own dreams of directing a film required her to return to it. Just as Steedman found when reflecting on female emancipation that 'we could not have talked of escape except within a literary framework' (2005: 15), so Gerwig talks of escape within a cinematic framework that is semi-autobiographical and, as Chapter 3 explores, based on what is already established by the philosophy of Simone Weil, the essays of Joan Didion, the paintings of Wayne Thiebaud, the music of Alanis Morissette and the musical theatre of Stephen Sondheim.

For example and in conclusion, we might consider how Gerwig's onscreen task of going home again, recreating her youth and unpicking its culture actually hides its metaphorical meta-narrative in plain sight. To wit, Sondheim's *Merrily We Roll Along* (1981) is a telling choice for the annual St. Francis High School musical because its plot is a literal exploration of contrapuntal simultaneity. The show covers twenty years in the lives of three friends who get younger as the tale progresses with a young cast gradually shedding their ageing make-up and ending up in high school. Time and plot thus move in opposite directions: *Merrily We Roll Along* starts with its three characters in their thirties heading back into the past, becoming more idealistic, ambitious and in love the younger they get, until the show ends where *Lady Bird* begins, in high school, with the teenagers singing about their ambitions [see Figure 2.3]. Irony thus overwhelms the delicate structure of a work whose contrapuntal simultaneity proved too confusing for audiences to accept in its original production. Gerwig's script describes *Merrily We Roll Along* as '*actually a pretty upsetting and adult show*,' and yet it is an ideal model for her own film because watching Lady Bird become an adult as *Lady Bird* unfolds is inseparable from watching Gerwig, who is responsible for the unfolding of the film, returning to high school, thereby ensuring that 'both the new and the old environments are vivid, actual, occurring together contrapuntally' (Saïd 2001: 186). Such contrapuntal simultaneity deploys irony too, but subtly in order to avoid explicit autobiography. Gerwig moves the spotlight off herself, for example, when Lady Bird auditions for a part in *Merrily We Roll Along* with her imitation of a strident

Figure 2.3 Lady Bird in the chorus of Sondheim's *Merrily We Roll Along*

Barbra Streisand performing 'Everybody Says Don't' from Sondheim's *Anyone Can Whistle* (1964) and she fails to land a role. This rejection distinguishes Lady Bird from Gerwig because at that age Gerwig had won medals for her performances in musical theatre, had already performed in the school musical of Sondheim's *Into the Woods* (1986) and would doubtlessly have taken one of the main parts in *Merrily We Roll Along.* Thus Lady Bird diverges from Gerwig by turning her song's litany of prohibitions into a self-fulfilling prediction of failure: 'Everyone who auditioned got in. The part I got was basically not getting in.' While Gerwig gets to sing and dance in the spotlight, Lady Bird gets to clap in the darkness. As a spur to self-determination for a smart, young woman set upon transcending class and classes, however, not getting in might even be better than bagging a lead role, which would only have ruined *Lady Bird* by making her too close to Gerwig's girlhood to be unique in her own.

3 Love and Attention

Aesthetics and Feelings

Sister Sarah-Joan reads Lady Bird's college application essay and deduces 'you clearly love Sacramento':

LADY BIRD: I do?
SISTER SARAH-JOAN: Well, you write about Sacramento so affectionately, and with such care.
LADY BIRD: I was just describing it.
SISTER SARAH-JOAN: It comes across as love.
LADY BIRD: Sure, I guess I pay attention.
SISTER SARAH-JOAN: Don't you think maybe they are the same thing? Love and attention?

The nun's question derives not from Catholicism but from the practice of Transcendentalism as this aligns with the beliefs of the 20th-century mystic Simone Weil, who declared that 'attention, taken to its highest degree, is the same thing as prayer. It presupposes love' ([1947] 2002: 117). Weil defined paying attention as a contemplative practice that pays spiritual dividends with social benefits, an idea that Gerwig acknowledges as determinant in relation to *Lady Bird*: 'I think attention is a devotional act. Paying attention to a person, to a place, it can be an act of love, an act of devotion' (quoted in Asay 2017). Consequently, following this exchange, Gerwig holds a mid-shot of Lady Bird and the nun facing each other in profile before cutting to one for which we have been primed to pay attention:

INT. THRIFT TOWN. DAY

Marion and Lady Bird are looking for a prom dress, Lady Bird is in the dressing room trying things on.

DOI: 10.4324/9781003240907-4

Pay attention: as described in Chapter 1, the scene in the thrift store is an inter-generational contest of colours that deepens the theme of simultaneity in the mother-daughter relationship and multiplies it in mirrors. Marion wears plain blue scrubs and Lady Bird, wanting to be her own different person and seeing herself reflected in the mirror *and* in her mother, rejects a blue dress and chooses a '*bright pink and frilly*' one instead. But Marion, who is not ready to let her potentially post-feminist daughter grow up so fast, stands behind her and asks if the dress is '*too* pink?' [see Figure 3.1]. The problem is that neither mother nor daughter are paying enough attention to each other to like or truly love what they see, even though their simultaneity is colour-coded. Conversely, guided by the paintings of Wayne Thiebaud, the essays of Joan Didion, and the songs of Alanis Morissette, this chapter pays attention to the feeling of memory and the colour of experience. It thereby reveals the palette and the interplay of reflections that condition the aesthetic, inform the meaning, illustrate the conflict, and complicate the philosophy of *Lady Bird.* Accordingly, it examines how the philosophical praxis of Simone Weil coincides with methodologies for identifying and creating female spaces prescribed by Luce Irigaray. And it argues that the film resembles a prism through which different views of girlhood and Sacramento are possible, to the extent that it might include what Gilles Deleuze (2007) called crystal-images, which reveal the recreation of the past in a passing-present that points to a possible future.

Figure 3.1 'Is it *too* pink?' An inter-generational contest of colours

Nostalgia for Nostalgia

Is it possible to feel nostalgia for a time when it was possible to feel nostalgic? A gap of twenty years tends to separate filmmakers and their target audience from the youth cultures that are represented on film, as if two decades are essential for actual living memory to lapse enough for a fabricated idea of the past to take hold. This delaying strategy is how youth-focused films such as *Grease* (Kleiser, 1978) revives 1958, *Dirty Dancing* imitates 1963, *Dazed and Confused* (Linklater, 1993) resuscitates 1976 and *Mid-90s* (Hill, 2018) impersonates 1996, for example. Made in 2017, *Lady Bird* suggests a premature example of nostalgia for the first decade of the new century but its aesthetic is deflective. Instead of explicitly detailing Sacramento in 2002, the film looks back to the late 1960s and early 1970s in its deference to the palette of the paintings of Wayne Thiebaud and the observational strategy of the essays of Joan Didion, both of which celebrate the commonplace in ways that will only be recognised as profound by Lady Bird at the end of her film, when she recalls 'all those bends I've known my whole life, and stores, and the whole thing.' The bright colours and long shadows of *Lady Bird* come from Thiebaud, while the backlit and low-light intimacy of its interiors suggest the scrutiny of Didion. As the script discloses, however, Lady Bird at first '*resent*[s] *the stuck-ness of her own life*' in a place and time where life is stalled by the trauma of 9/11 and wary of the gathering storm of economic problems. Bothered by the uncanniness of the stasis and sensing the deflection of nostalgia, the first line of Lady Bird in *Lady Bird* is both the character and the film asking: 'Do you think I look like I'm from Sacramento?'

Later, in response to frustration with her own in-betweenness, Lady Bird declares 'I wish I could *live* through something' and thereby provides an ironic ambition for the film of her own name [see Figure 3.2]. Looking forward, it suggests the film will be mundane, yet this ambition actually looks backwards because Lady Bird aspires to live in a time and place when 'writers live in the woods,' which refers specifically to the two years (1845–47) that Henry David Thoreau lived in a cabin at Walden Pond in Concord, Massachusetts. She therefore declares herself a budding Transcendentalist in admiration of Thoreau, who spent his time in Walden Pond paying attention to nature, reflecting upon spirituality and learning to love his own capacity for self-determination by means of civil disobedience and the human potential for transcendence that resulted. And when that ambition is blocked by her mother – 'How in the world did I raise such a SNOB?' – Lady Bird '*dramatically opens the door and rolls out of the car.*'

Figure 3.2 Lady Bird wishing she could live through something

In a film about 'stuck-ness,' Lady Bird ejecting herself from the moving car allows for a playful reading of the rest of the film as following her waking up the next day like Marty McFly (Michael J. Fox) in the Hill Valley, California, of 1955 in *Back to the Future* (Zemeckis, 1985); except in Lady Bird's Sacramento it seems as if *The Graduate* (Nichols, 1967) is playing at the local cinema and Joan Didion is still writing for the *Saturday Evening Post*. Clues to her time travel are insistent. Lady Bird is shown twice hunting for vintage clothes at the thrift store as if emulating Marty McFly in having to dress herself more fittingly for an earlier time, although she complicates this tactic with a layering of times in her outfits, thereby revealing an attempt at self-determination that is wavering between the past, present and future. The far-away war in Iraq carries reminders of that in Vietnam and when Lady Bird is confronted by a poster of Ronald Reagan in Danny's grandmother's house and asks, 'is this…a joke?,' Gerwig inverts the scene in *Back to the Future* when Doc Brown (Christopher Lloyd) tests Marty's knowledge of the future and scoffs when Marty tells him Reagan is president. Thus, following the model of Sondheim's *Merrily We Roll Along*, Gerwig re-visits her high school in the making of *Lady Bird* by ironically recreating an era in which Lady Bird only wants to go *further* back in time to one in which Sacramento is less troubled, softly aglow in the paintings of Thiebaud and more meaningful in the writings of Didion. Consequently, her time machine is not a DeLorean but the film's aesthetics, which deflect nostalgia for 2002 to the late 1960s and early 1970s. This is partly because Lady Bird is adrift in post-9/11 and pre-crash America, and partly because the fifteen-year gap between its audience in 2017 and its setting of 2002–03 is premature and has done nothing yet to inspire or justify nostalgic feelings for a time when dread was endemic. Indeed, the first decade of the 21st century has been unmasked in the #MeToo era as particularly injurious to any nostalgia that women might feel for these years in which teenage female icons such as Britney Spears, Lindsey Lohan (Cady in *Mean Girls*), Brittany Murphy (Tai in *Clueless*) and countless young women were, as is now known, actually abused and fearful. As the priest declares in his sermon heard over the opening credits: 'We're afraid we won't get into the college of our choice, we're afraid we won't be loved, we won't be liked, we won't succeed.' Reading *Lady Bird* as a film about the self-determination for a new century of young women thus requires recognition of its strategy of denial, blocking, disassociation and deferral that is typical of the traumatised, as well as the film's movement towards reconciliation, relief and hope.

To an extent, this strategy in *Lady Bird* recasts the performative ennui of its teenagers and their misplaced nostalgia as a therapeutic deflection. Stunned and scared, open about their distaste for 2002–03 and evasive about the responsibilities that await them in adulthood, they already know not to trust new technology and the government:

KYLE: You don't have a cell phone?
LADY BIRD: Nah.
KYLE: Good girl. The government didn't have to put tracking devices on us, we bought them and put them on ourselves.

But the film also emphasises that all generations are suffering equally and that the typical lack of communication between them exacerbates suffering on all sides. When a crying Danny admits his homosexuality to Lady Bird, Gerwig cuts from a shot of her comforting him – '*He's telling the truth and she is genuinely touched. They embrace again. They are friends, real friends now*' – to one of her mother simultaneously extending sympathy to Father Leviatch (Stephen McKinley Henderson), '*who looks how he feels - crushed by bottomless despair*' as he checks into her psychiatric hospital:

MARION: …and do you have a support system?
FATHER LEVIATCH: What do you mean?
MARION: (*gently*) Who do you turn to when you feel this way?

FATHER LEVIATCH: No one, I guess. I'm sorry.
MARION: No, no, don't be sorry. There's no wrong answer.
She looks at him with true empathy. He realises something.
FATHER LEVIATCH: Please don't tell your daughter.
MARION: No of course not. Of course not.

The cut insists on what has already been posited as the unwitting simultaneity of mother and daughter, who both warrant Danny's description of Marion as 'warm but also kinda scary.' But the juxtaposition also emphasises the increasing isolation of all characters in the new century. Jenna's great-aunt just killed herself, Kyle's father is dying of cancer, and Larry's friend of the same age has just died. Lady Bird is not alone in wanting to live in a gentler time.

The Colour of Memory

Nostalgia is a false cure for a dispiriting present because it exacerbates the sense that things will never be as good as they were before. It is launched from the passing-present to a past that is reimagined to suit the true purpose of this nostalgia, which is to bounce an idea of the past into the future as succour, target and reward. Making Sacramento great again is about refilling it with the frothy sodas and creamy desserts of the paintings of Wayne Thiebaud, whose work is indelibly identified with the city in the late 1960s and 1970s. Thiebaud attended Sacramento State College (now California State College, Sacramento) and taught at Sacramento Junior College (now Sacramento City College). He held the first of eight solo exhibitions in Sacramento's Crocker Art Museum in 1951, founded the Sacramento Artist's Cooperative in 1958 and always believed that 'to be local is the touchstone of what you are and where you come from, what you are seeing' (Jones and Shields 2020: 6). His art echoed Simone Weil and the Transcendentalists in being 'based on observation and convincingly executed. [It] looks real and often feels comfortingly familiar, qualities that have led most viewers to describe it as realist' (7). But look closer and look again in an approach that Scott A. Shields calls 'extended looking' because:

> At the same time, extended looking acknowledges the works' artifice, as Thiebaud filters it through his memory, knowledge of art history, and imagination, making it possible, as he states 'for representational painting to be both abstract and real simultaneously.' (2020a: 9)

Between Abstract Expressionism (Mark Rothko, Jackson Pollock, Clyfford Still) and Pop Art (Jasper Johns, Roy Lichtenstein, Robert Rauschenberg), Thiebaud makes his desserts with bold strokes of paint that become the cream and jam, literally caking it on. 'Pies, Pies, Pies' (1961) and 'Boston Cremes' (1962) invite the viewer to stick a finger into any or all of the desserts lined up on the diner's counter (see bibliography for links to images of mentioned works). The stark, commercial, fluorescent lighting kindles sickliness but this is processed food from diners and movie theatres that factors an early glut into the exchange. 'Strawberry Cone' (1969) is an uncanny, almost absurd, possibly surreal simultaneity of form (paint) and content (ice cream) that, like the bold primary colours and messaging of advertising in this era, invites, even demands one try a lick. Thiebaud's custard and meringue are so sensual that they resemble cartoons without losing their place in the real word because shading, perspective and textures act like anchors. Paint *is* ice cream, ketchup and a banana split. Bread *is* white and coffee *is* brown and mustard *is* yellow. These are edible colours to be consumed by extended looking and only the basic composition rescues them from abstraction. In all senses, these paintings are confectionery, constructed to make processed food reach its Proustian potential. 'Buffet' (1972–75) is a table spread that looks like a fairground: the trifle is a tent, a three-tier tray of sandwiches is a helter-skelter. Thus, 'extended looking' by the artist inspires 'extended looking' by the viewer because 'Thiebaud lures his viewers into believing that what he presents is real, at least until extended looking reveals the hoax' (Shields 2020a: 17). This exchange resembles a ritual, being contrived, promising transcendence like the copy on an advertisement for just such a spread in *Better Living* magazine. Thiebaud paints low-income foods, 'foods most Americans have eaten and, on average, can afford. [...] American sandwich bread as opposed to a French baguette, for example' (Shields 2020b: 34). The colour of memory is bright, affordable and filling.

Thiebaud paints people too, but differently. There is no invitation to touch in 'Two Seated Figures' (1965a) in which the man and woman have their arms tightly folded and are looking away in opposite directions. Indeed, there is often a huffy lack of communication between his humans: his 'Swimsuit Figures' (1965b) stand as if in a queue: the woman, again with arms folded, stands a step ahead of the man whose gaze is fixed on something ahead and above them both, such as a list of ice-cream flavours. Solitary female figures in 'Tapestry Skirt' (1976) and 'Betty Jean Thiebaud and Book' (1965–69) are both engaged in extended looking at the artist, but there is tension in the clasped hands of the first and the fingers reaching for the temple of the second. These are women as Luce Irigaray supposes them, silent, private and bothered. Betty Jane Thiebaud, the filmmaker wife of the artist, appears throughout his paintings of the 1960s in a range of reproachful poses, such as that in 'Betty Jean Thiebaud and Book' in which her husband painting her is seemingly distracting her from reading. Her gaze complies with the task while waiting to connect with that of other women in a more private way. (If anything is missing from *Lady Bird* it is a scene in which mother and daughter bin their ice-cream cones as they wander into the Crocker Art Museum in Sacramento to stand before this very painting in which their gaze might be triangulated with that of Betty Jean). Thiebaud's women are emphatic in not letting their being painted define them in works such as 'Bikini' (1964) and 'Tapestry Skirt' in which their costuming is not belittling but weaponised by a defiant gaze. Lady Bird makes a similar effort with the customisation of her school uniform and when released from it wears a mix of simple items and thrift-store finds, smart combinations of vintage, post-grunge, late punk and pre-hipster chic that pull off cool by accident (with credit due to April Napier, who also dressed the teens in *Booksmart*) [see Figure 3.3]. In *Lady Bird*'s final scene in New York in 2003, there is even a touch of *Annie Hall* (Allen, 1977) about her flared jeans and slightly outsized jacket, which recalls too Thiebaud's 'Girl in Striped Blouse' (1973–76) in pose and demeanour, while overlapping times and cycles are shown in such items as the flared trousers, which are redolent of the 1970s but were back in fashion in the early

Figure 3.3 A holdover from grunge and a punk throwback...

Figure 3.4 ...with a touch of *Annie Hall*

2000s [see Figure 3.4]. For special occasions like Thanksgiving and the school prom, Lady Bird visits the time machine of the thrift store and tries on dresses worn by previous generations until she finds those that pull off vintage cool. Transcendence is in the details as well as in the grand Romantic gesture that they all add up to, with *Lady Bird* inviting its audience to engage in a strategy of extended looking (Thiebaud) that includes paying attention (Weil) and looking again (Irigaray).

Lady Bird is a prism that refracts the light and colour of various iterations of Sacramento. Turning the prism confirms that *Lady Bird* constructs nostalgia *for* nostalgia, pitting living memory in 2017 against the fabrication of 2002–03 and ideas encased in amber of the 1970s. This layering questions the moral and ethical value of nostalgia in relation to representations of youth cultures that might be edified or betrayed by such biased cocooning of the past and the extension of this fiction into the future. As an indicator of the mindset of those in 2002–03 by those in 2017, *Lady Bird*'s recourse to nostalgia for the 1960s–70s is complex and contradictory. What Gerwig takes from Thiebaud is not just the light and colour of Sacramento in the 1960s and 1970s but a profound sense of the plasticity of nostalgia. This malleable quality extends to urban landscapes and the people in them too as these appear manufactured: nature is tamed, trained, fenced in and cemented over, perspective is manipulated and the direction of light is plotted. Thiebaud's Sacramento seems prefabricated for its reuse by Gerwig, who, according to production designer Chris Jones, 'used Thiebaud as a starting point, and we just ran with that' (quoted in

Malkin 2018). Thiebaud's paintings frame and flatten the city as if it were the subject of cartoons in *The Saturday Evening Post* or matte paintings for the animated adventures of a teenage superhero called Lady Bird. But there is depth here too. These are not the ice-cream colours of a Wes Anderson film; these are ice-cream flavours. Thiebaud paints shadows in order to paint the light, which is 'omnipresent in Sacramento, where light radiates heat' (Shields 2020b: 40). He lays it on as lightly, lucidly and tangibly as the great Valencian artist Joaquín Sorolla, whose paintings illuminate Gerwig's filming of the scene at the beach in *Little Women*. Indeed, 'some of the strongest and deepest colours in Thiebaud's paintings are to be found in his shadows, which he studied under Sacramento's scorching sun' (ibid.). The deep textures on shallow planes in his paintings of food, drink and cosmetics have an intensity that resembles the haptics of dreaming. Indeed, this oneiric quality is an essential factor in the confection of nostalgia and it extends to the rendition of characters in *Lady Bird* too because the placement of human figures in painting, literature and film can, as Steedman states, convey a 'social understanding [that] helps interpret the dream landscape' (2005: 143).

Like Weil paying attention and Irigaray asking us to look again, Thiebaud's extended looking 'draws upon a combination of perception and memory to create paintings that bring common objects and common experiences to our attention in ways that we had not imagined' (Markle Lovell 2020: 59). Thus, the self-determination of objects like a strawberry cone and of characters like Lady Bird are performed as a breakthrough in perception on the flat canvasses of the countertop and the background of Sacramento respectively. Indeed, because 'Thiebaud surrounded his figures with halations of colour to enliven and counterbalance the stasis of their poses and to connect them with the surrounding space in insignificant – and often liminal – moments' (43), so several images of Lady Bird in the early morning or late afternoon, including that of her in a white t-shirt and tartan pinafore standing with her back against the wall of the convenience store, replicate the bold textures on a flat surface that typify the work of Thiebaud [see Figure 3.5]. Such images, like the paintings of Thiebaud, ask the same question as Steedman in *Landscape for a Good Woman*:

> Where is the place that you move into the landscape and can see yourself? [...] To see yourself in this way is a representation of the child's move into historical time, one of the places where vision establishes the child's understanding of herself as part of the world.
> (2005: 142–3)

Figure 3.5 Lady Bird performs self-determination on the flat canvas of Sacramento

Here Steedman provides the key to understanding Lady Bird by defining self-determination as something that will only be achieved when Lady Bird moves into a landscape in which she can see herself apart from her mother. To wit, Lady Bird's self-determination depends upon her getting away from the glow of Sacramento to the harsh light of the East Coast. For a film that is tinged, taunted and even tainted by nostalgia, *Lady Bird* contrasts Thiebaud's thick and creamy brushstrokes with Steedman's surgical diagnosis of the potentially malignant effects of nostalgia on childhood: 'You're nostalgic for childhood whilst it's happening to you, because the dreams show you the landscape you're passing through, but you don't know yet that you want to escape' (2005: 143). Not yet.

Refractions of Sacramento

As suggested, seeing *Lady Bird* as a prism through which ideas, memories and experiences of Sacramento are refracted suggests correspondence with the 'crystals of time' theorised by Gilles Deleuze (2007: 66–94). In the crystal-image 'there is a formation of an image with two sides, actual and virtual […] following a double movement of liberation and capture' (66–7). Thus, the 'actual' side of *Lady Bird* is presented as 2002–03, while its 'virtual' side is the nostalgic vision of Sacramento in the early 1970s that affects this present and informs the psychological realism of the film itself. Both actual and virtual are simultaneous in the film, making for the 'indiscernibility of the real and the imaginary, or of the present and the past' (68). To some extent, moreover, because *Lady Bird* deliberately confuses nostalgia for the Sacramento of 2002–03 with nostalgia for the Sacramento of the early 1970s, the film foregrounds simultaneity in resembling 'present and past, still present and already past, at once and at the same time' (76). In this respect, *Lady Bird* resembles *Frances Ha*, in which 21st-century New York resembles 1960s' Paris, meaning it 'seems simultaneously very old and very new. So does its protagonist. Frances lives in 2013, and yet she refracts cinematic light from 1959 and 1964 and 1986' (Baker 2013: 14). As examined in Chapter 1, simultaneity is prevalent in the dynamic of mother and daughter too, but mapping their central conflict on the confluence of times sees Lady Bird as the frustrated present, her mother as the burdensome past, and their reconciliation in a yet-to-happen future that only Larry, the husband/father, can perceive:

LADY BIRD: (*looking down*): Does Mom hate me?
LARRY: You both have such…strong personalities. She doesn't know how to help you and that frustrates her.
LADY BIRD: I wish she'd talk to me.
LARRY: She will, I know.

The drama of *Lady Bird* is this split between mother and daughter although, as Deleuze surmises, 'time consists of this split, and it is this, it is time, that we *see in the crystal*' (2007: 79, italics in the original). In accordance with Deleuze, the fact that mother and daughter differ from each other in nature 'split[s] the present in two heterogenous directions, one of which is launched towards the future while the other falls into the past' (ibid.). Thus, turning the crystal (watching the film) creates a centrifugal force that splits mother and daughter apart while simultaneously constructing a future that contains the possibility of their centripetal reunion. Indeed, watching the film (turning the crystal) reveals that for all their differences, daughter and mother are simultaneously strong personalities who as yet lack cognisance of a reconciliation that only Larry continues to see as inevitable:

Marion drives away abruptly. Lady Bird gets smaller in the frame. Marion is the focus. Marion circles, then circles back. She is crying now, she thought it would be easier to not say goodbye but it isn't. She parks the car. Runs as fast as she can to go say goodbye. Runs into the airport looking for Lady Bird and Larry. Sees Larry walking towards her.
LARRY (*hugging her while she cries*): It's ok, she'll be back, she'll come back.

Correlatively, the crystal of *Lady Bird* is one in which perception of our 'passing-present' (in which we are watching the film in 2017 or since) splits too, revealing the passing-*film*-present of 2002–03 that is represented onscreen, as well as the passing-*film*-past of the early 1970s that is suggested by the film's aesthetics. *Lady Bird*'s content and mise-en-scène (clothes, cars, music, etc.) and its aesthetics and form (colour, lighting, tone, etc.) are by no means rigidly categorised, separable or inseparable; rather they are mobile and transparent, giving *Lady Bird* the layered look and feel of a memory that resembles Sacramento in 2002–03, albeit blended with the nostalgia felt by someone living in Sacramento at that time for the 1970s. The film's simulacrum of the beginning of the new century is thus partly a palimpsest of a previous time, which is real for Marion, who lived it, and simultaneously virtual for Lady Bird, who experiences nostalgia for a time when she was not yet born. All told, this layering effects a shimmering in the crystal-image that complies with the 'confusion of the real and the imaginary [that] is produced solely in someone's head' (Deleuze 2007: 67).

Nostalgia tends to confuse the real past with an imaginary one. That a film made in 2017 should struggle to justify nostalgia for the reality of 2002–03 and deflect this onto an imagined 1970s emphasises how premature is the sentiment. But it also signals how 2002–03 was a period of dread, particularly for low-income families, that inspired their looking back to better times, which would soon be exploited by the Make America Great Again campaign of Donald Trump. This displacement of nostalgia for 2002–03 to the 1970s also responds to how life in the 21st century can suffer 'stuck-ness' because perception of the sublime is hindered by our attention being occupied by the trivial. Since the beginning of the 21st century, disastrous climate change has been bearing down on our own lifetimes, a pandemic has raged across the globe, and overpopulation is fuelling environmental, economic and humanitarian crises; yet the distractions of social media have been simultaneous, compressing anger, anxiety, compassion and activism into fleeting engagements with the apocalypse. In *Lady Bird*, however, looking back to the 1970s is a comforting distraction that does not postpone the movement of Lady Bird's debt-ridden family towards the economic crisis of 2008. Nostalgia is palliative care, aimed at enhancing the quality of life and mitigating suffering for those with serious, complex, worsening problems of debt.

The blend of times is the end of times in *Lady Bird*. 2002–03 is onscreen in the fashion and cars that were around then but getting older for those who could not afford to renew, while the 1970s are prevalent in references to Thiebaud, Didion and Sondheim. Historical facts that might anchor or sort the allusions are only glimpsed, however, with the Vietnam-like war in Iraq flickering briefly on television screens before Lady Bird is distracted. First by a phone call:

INT. LADY BIRD'S HOUSE. EARLY AFTERNOON.

Lady Bird lounging - watching television. Life during Suspension. All these reports about the lead up to the Iraq war. It's simultaneously terrifying and boring. The phone rings and she JUMPS at it.

And then by mail a few days later:

INT. LADY BIRD'S HOUSE. DAY.

Lady Bird is back to watching television. The invasion is full on, it's the Shock and Awe portion of the Iraq war.
MIGUEL: Lady Bird! A bunch of things arrived for you!
Lady Bird rushes in, snatches the envelopes from his hand.

In both scenes the war onscreen is disregarded, which is arguably less indicative of disinterest than trauma resulting from 9/11 and the self-serving blockage of further psychological aggressions. Indeed, there are few mentions of 9/11 in the film, which happened less than a year before Lady Bird begins her 2002–03 school year, and this only serves to point up the solipsism of Lady Bird, who admits to exploiting the national trauma for her college application:

LADY BIRD: Mom. Mom. Aren't you sort of proud that I'm so close to getting in? Just a little?
Follows Marion to the backyard, where she begins weeding.
LADY BIRD: I mean, yes, I know it was probably easier because 9/11 and less people applying with terrorism and all that, still though … I'm sorry, I know I can lie and not be a good person but…

Nostalgia for 2002–03 is simply elsewhere, locked into a strategy of avoidance, of looking away from the present in the opposite direction to a threatening future, towards a past that always has better music.

Statements of Feeling

In films about youth cultures, songs are often bound to the collective identity of rockers, mods, greasers, punks and the like, while in coming-of-age films, which aim to pinpoint specific moments in time with a needle drop, the redolent soundtrack collection has become a genre trope with marketing potential since *American Graffiti* (Lucas, 1973). But whereas young men singing tend towards unrehearsed public extroversion, young women more often sing in practiced groups and flounder. Boys that triumph by being extravagantly spontaneous include Patrick Verona (Heath Ledger) performing with the accompaniment of a marching band in *10 Things I Hate About You*, Ferris Bueller (Matthew Broderick) commandeering a parade to celebrate his best friend in *Ferris Bueller's Day Off* (Hughes, 1986) and Tom (Joseph Gordon-Levitt) expressing post-coital bliss in *(500) Days of Summer* (Webb, 2009) by performing with a flash mob. Girls on the other hand seek and express solidarity in collective, rehearsed performances, as cheerleaders in *Bring It On* (Reed, 2000), dance troupes in *Work It* (Terruso, 2020) and acapella groups in *Pitch Perfect* (Moore, 2012), and their performances, moreover, tend to go wrong. The boombox cuts out in *Mean Girls*, the troupe collapses in *It Felt Like Love* and several performances implode throughout the *Pitch Perfect* franchise. So whereas boys tend to be show-offs, girls are more committed to collective and individual acts of self-determination that have to overcome obstacles as well as prejudice. Only rarely does female spontaneity flourish outright and then only privately, as when the four young women affirm their collective identity by singing Rihanna's 'Diamonds' in a hotel room in *Bandes des filles* (Girlhood) (Sciamma, 2014). Otherwise, individual expression is either subdued in response to failure, such as when Beca (Anna Kendrick) leaves the spotlight and sits cross-legged at the edge of the stage to perform her audition in *Pitch Perfect*, or surprises even the performer, such as in *Booksmart* when Amy steps up to the karaoke machine to belt out 'She Oughta Know' by Alanis Morissette.

Morissette received one of three pleading letters written by Gerwig to secure songs that she deemed crucial to the mindset of her semi-autobiographical protagonist. The one to Justin Timberlake declares 'your rise corresponded exactly with my very awkward puberty' and requests the rights to 'Cry Me A River' (2002), which Gerwig plays over Lady Bird and Kyle 'when they full on make out' because it is 'what "Gimme Shelter" must have felt like to the kids of the late 60s' (Gerwig 2021: 183). Timberlake's song is thus redolent of the aural crystal because it evokes the passing-present of the film while adding a possible future in illustration of Gerwig's belief that 'I think that when you're a teenager, music is the way you try to imagine the future [and] what it would be like to be in love, to go on a road trip, to have wild adventures, to create art, to be a person in the world' (179). Indeed,

Gerwig invokes simultaneity in writing these letters by admitting that 'I wish I could go back in time and tell my sixteen-year-old self that this moment was coming – she'd never believe me, but truth be told, my thirty-two-year-old self hardly can believe it either' (ibid.).

Gerwig's second letter asks Dave Matthews for 'Crash into Me' (1996), which she mis-remembers as 'the most romantic song ever' (2021: 179) because it is actually creepy, written from the perspective of an adolescent Peeping Tom. But this only corroborates Richard Dyer's assertion that a song is 'a particularly rich semiotic mix for the statement of feeling' (Dyer 2012: 5). Indeed, when Dyer asserts that 'song, like all art, is at the intersection between individual feelings and the socially and historically specific shared forms available to express that feeling' (2), he points to how songs can function diegetically as markers of period and symbols of plot-based feeling as well as non-diegetically as borrowed commentary or second-hand illustration of internalised emotion. *Lady Bird* contains and reveals this aural intersection between (internal) psychology and (external) society as a crystalline contrast between non-diegetic songs playing inside Lady Bird's head and the diegetic songs (sometimes the same ones) that she hears around her. For example, as Gerwig explains to Dave Matthews, 'Crash into Me' appears twice: 'First in a heartbroken, yearning moment of teenage pain' expressing her anguish over breaking up with Danny, which starts diegetically on the cassette player in her car and continues non-diegetically over her refusing to hold hands with Danny at the curtain-call, and 'then later, it's used as <u>the</u> turning point when our heroine comes into her own, declares her love for the song and what she actually cares about in life' (Gerwig 2021: 179), which is when the song appears diegetically on the car radio and is scorned by Kyle, prompting Lady Bird to abandon him on prom night. For Lady Bird, as for Deleuze, 'time itself becomes a thing of sound' (2007: 91) with the result that the complex interplay of songs includes those of her era and those of her ego: two sound waves, one actual and one virtual, spiralling together like two ribbons of different colours.

The use of songs to evoke emotional and identitary complexity is a staple of the coming-of-age film. In the London-set *Bend it Like Beckham* (Chadha, 2002), the challenges of integration faced by Jess (Parminder Nagra) are illustrated by a mix of aspirational 'Girl Power' songs in English with Bhangra and Asian Underground music in Punjabi and Hindi, while in *It Felt Like Love* the brutally misogynistic lyrics of pounding hip-hop are what goad the emotionally ill-equipped Lila into a fearful bluff of sexual experience. *Lady Bird* has its own rich mix to cope with its protagonist's myriad feelings that includes hymns ('Rosa Mystica,' 'Panis Angelicus' and 'Prayer of St. Francis'), brief instrumental tracks by Jon Brion ('Lady Bird Kiss' is the longest at 105 seconds), a medley of Sondheim tunes performed at the high school musical auditions, and an essential anthem by Morissette. Indeed, Gerwig's letter to Morissette is her most gushing: 'I have been a fan of yours my whole life. Your music helped to define my entire adolescence. [...] You made a lot of girls feel like they could do anything' (2021: 181). Accordingly, the prominence in female-centred, coming-of-age dramas of songs by Morissette is because they recognise, affirm and anthemise the contradictions that make up the experiences and identities of young women such as the protagonists of *Lady Bird*, *Booksmart*, *The Craft: Legacy* (Lister-Jones, 2020), *Dawson's Creek* and *Glee* (Fox, 2009–15).

'Hand in My Pocket' was to have been the theme song for the pilot episode of *Dawson's Creek* until Morissette refused its use and remained unrelenting until its use in Season Six (see Kaplan 2018). It was also covered in the third episode of Season Six of *Glee* entitled 'Jagged Little Tapestry' as a sapphic duet between Santana (Naya Rivera) and Brittany (Heather Morris) that was also a mash-up with Carole King's 'I Feel the Earth Move' and the prelude to Santana proposing they get married. Morissette is also emblematic of the female-centred, coming-of-age film for the aforementioned scene in *Booksmart* where Amy grabs the karaoke microphone and *owns* her Morissette-ish hair with a rendition of 'You Oughta Know.' In her letter, Gerwig tells Morissette that 'your music helped to define my entire adolescence' (2021: 181) and her use of 'Hand in My Pocket' encapsulates Lady Bird's contradictions: caring but restless, here but gone, sad but laughing, brave but chicken shit. These lyrics capture what Handyside has termed 'the paradoxes of the postfeminist subject – passive and active; girly but determined; trivial pursuits and serious intent; fragility and drive; naturalness and artifice' (2017: 34). Indeed, like 'Crash into Me,' the song appears diegetically when '*Lady Bird and Larry* [are] *on the way to school. She feverishly changes the radio station, finds a song she likes*' and then continues non-diegetically when she gets out of the family's Toyota Corolla early to avoid embarrassment and walks the last block to school. Documenting her mix of pretension and inadequacy, her certainty and unease, her agency and inertia, her phenomenology and her potential for transcendence, the song captures and releases all those contradictions that are explained by the philosophy of Simone Weil, who wrote on 'the two forces that rule the universe: light and gravity' and aimed to resolve this duality by accepting that 'the links that we cannot forge are evidence of the transcendent' ([1947] 2002: 1, 95).

According to Weil, the struggle to reconcile the kind of offbeat opposites grasped by Morissette is not resolved by submission to victimhood nor triumphalism in any form but in recognising the meaning of the struggle itself because, ultimately, 'nothing in the world can rob us of the power to say "I"' ([1947] 2002: 26). That is to say, self-determination can only come from struggle, which is necessary because 'it is only affliction which makes us feel this' (94). As Weil states and Morissette insists, we are the sum of our contradictions and our aim should be 'by dint of patience, effort and method to come to understand with our whole self the truths which are evident' (116). Thus, on closer listening, 'Hand in My Pocket' does not identify antonyms nor contradictions but conditions that exude simultaneity, showing that one can care, be here, laughing and brave and, at the same time, be restless, gone, sad and chicken shit too. The song thus encapsulates the physical and psychological bargaining by the ego between the id and the super-ego in its chorus, which heralds simple, personally meaningful acts of self-affirmation – givin' a high five and flickin' a cigarette – that symbolise self-determination and the potential of smart young women to achieve transcendence.

Something in Our Soul

The attention Gerwig pays to songs aligns with Simone Weil's 'method for understanding images, symbols, etc, [which is] not to try to interpret them, but to look at them till the light suddenly dawns' ([1947] 2002: 120). Weil counsels 'absolutely unmixed attention in prayer' (117) and teaches, as Lady Bird learns eventually, that love and attention are the same thing. For Weil, moreover, *not* paying attention to life is what brings forth evil: 'That is why every time that we really concentrate our attention, we destroy the evil in ourselves' (62). Accordingly, it might be noted that a major change between the time shown in the film (2002–03) and that of its release (2017) is social media, which has arguably contributed to a reduction in attention spans (less than 280 characters for a tweet and no more than three minutes for TikTok). As Gerwig stated in 2017, 'to be dealing with teenagers now you have to shoot cell phones, and so much of their lives happens online, and I don't think it's very cinematic. I felt like in a weird way this was the last generation you could make a film about without doing that' (quoted in Harvey 2017). Is *Lady Bird* therefore a portrait of youth at the last time they paid attention to something that was not on a handheld screen, and thus the last time that their potential for transcendence was possible?

For Weil as for Lady Bird, the act of paying attention is training in the act of love and it resembles too the Transcendentalist practice advocated by Thoreau, who took himself off to Walden Pond for two years in order to 'live deliberately, to front only the essential facts of life, and see if I could not learn what it had to teach' ([1854] 2004: 97). In his endeavour, Thoreau prefigured Weil's subscription to paying attention as a means of reaching a state of being in which 'our thought should be empty, waiting, not seeking anything, but ready to receive in its naked truth the object that is to penetrate it' ([1951] 2009: 62). The outcome, as Thoreau discovered, Weil surmised and Sister Sarah-Joan informs Lady Bird, is that 'we cannot contemplate without a certain love. The contemplation of the image of the order of the world constitutes a certain contact with the beauty of the world' (Weil [1951] 2009: 108). Indeed, this connection to filmmaking, which is based on contemplation of the image, is vital to Gerwig, who dedicates two pages to Weil in the broadsheet A24 zine that she edited entitled 'Lady Saints and Mystics' (2017), a compilation of religious art, poetry and an editor's letter in which Gerwig declares:

> I'm interested in what women do in spaces that are primarily male, in structures that are patriarchal. Most religions and religious institutions fall into this category. Priesthood and direct communion with God is generally reserved for men. But then, every so often, a woman, usually a young woman, hears directly from God, or talks to the Virgin Mary, or is overcome by something mysterious and terrifying and beautiful. All of the hierarchies of gender are bypassed. She is possessed by piercing truth and awe. (2017: 3)

Born into a Jewish family in Paris in 1909, Weil was a philosopher who would have been labelled a mystic in earlier centuries and a feminist in recent decades. Her forceful writing reinstated the womb in religious thought and thereby contributed to a gynocentric religiosity that confronted the Catholic Church of the 20th century with its own paradox as a religion centred on the virginal/maternal figure of Mary that tends to oppress women. In this Weil aligns with Irigaray, who 'appeals to her readers to take images of woman, such as the Virgin Mary, and rethink these figures in a new way: for example, images of Mary with her mother [to suggest] a new symbolic representation of women [and] a suitable recognition of maternal genealogy' (Bolton 2015: 57). Weil rethought and reconfigured what modern women could do by the example of her own actions, joining trades unions and strikes, fighting on the side of the anarchists in the Spanish Civil War, becoming active in the French Resistance during World War Two, and engaging in correspondence with the likes of Trotsky and notable German communists fleeing the rise of Fascism. But she was sickly too and extremely short-sighted, which saw her rejected by the Spanish Republican forces for being unable to shoot a rifle or manage a machine-gun. She held her own grand Romantic gestures to be graceless and ineffective until her efforts at self-determination gained focus through her experience of aesthetic pleasures and even ecstasy in Catholic rituals, which empowered her interest in mysticism. Like Lady Bird and Gerwig in high school, however, Weil was non-Catholic in a Catholic context: she disregarded the paraphernalia of Catholicism, such as the Eucharist, and therefore did not participate in communion, holding that, while 'it is almost impossible to distinguish faith from its social imitation[,] Christ can be present in such an object only by convention' ([1951] 2009: 122, 129). This allowed her to dissect the myriad elements of what she observed and thereby approach transcendence by means of paying attention, which means 'holding in our minds, within reach of this [subjective] thought, but on a lower level and not in contact with it, the diverse [objective] knowledge we have acquired, which we are forced to make use of' (62).

This devotional act of paying attention and reasoning was a skill Weil claimed to have acquired from time spent on 'school exercises [which] only deliver a lower kind of attention' ([1951] 2009: 57):

> If we have no aptitude or natural taste for geometry, this does not mean that our faculty for attention will not be developed by wrestling with a problem or studying a theorem. […] Without our knowing or feeling it, this apparently barren effort has brought more light into the soul.
>
> (57–8)

This explains why Sister Sarah-Joan questions Lady Bird's aptitude for mathematics and Lady Bird says she would 'really like to be on Math Olympiad [the World Championship Mathematics Competition for high school students]' regardless, thereby illustrating a crucial element of Weil's belief system and how much Lady Bird resembles her. Indeed, page six of Gerwig's A24 zine has a photo of a youthful Weil looking not unlike Saoirse Ronan as Lady Bird and a brief biography opposite two extracts from her letters: the first declares the Catholic Church to be a confusing, even dangerous social structure, and the second describes what sounds like typical teenage angst: 'At fourteen I fell into one of those fits of bottomless despair that come with adolescence, and I seriously thought of dying because of the mediocrity of my natural faculties' (quoted in Gerwig 2017: 7). But Weil found a way through adolescence that depended on finding the connection between paying attention and love, a revelation visited on Lady Bird in her essay on Sacramento and in the film's final scene. This aligns Lady Bird with the lady saints and mystics featured in Gerwig's zine, of whom she states:

> They are odd and funny and specific – teenage girls who hear God (or want to), women who write journals or poetry, women who struggle with faith, women who died for their beliefs. They inspire me, primarily, to listen. Listening is the most important task of any actor, but also of directors and writers. Because when you grow quiet, there is a chance, however unlikely, that something divine will speak to you and through you.
>
> (2017: 3)

Thus the act of devotion that Thoreau and Weil exhort and is enacted by Lady Bird in writing her essay is also that of Gerwig in making her film, which joins the paintings of Thiebaud and the essays of Didion in paying close and loving attention to Sacramento.

Slouching towards Sacramento

'Slouching towards Bethlehem' (1968) is the title for a collection of essays that Didion took from W.B. Yeats but is more aptly explained by this description of Simone Weil: 'Surely no "friend of God" in all history had moved more unwillingly toward the mystic encounter' (Fiedler 2009: viii). Indeed, the practice of paying attention that Weil bequeathes to Gerwig, who passes it on to Lady Bird, is equally indebted to Didion's aforementioned counterplay to rushing into hagiography and accepting the histories of others. The attention paid to Sacramento by Didion and Gerwig also heeds Weil's assertion that 'human cities in particular, each one more or less according to its degree of perfection, surround the life of their inhabitants with poetry' ([1951] 2009: 116). The result of paying attention to the details of one's world is not only love, however, but an exhausting awareness of human inconsequentiality, thereby confirming for Weil that it was 'the proper method of philosophy [which] consists in clearly conceiving the insoluble problems in all their insolubility and then in simply contemplating them, fixedly and tirelessly, year after year, without any hope, patiently waiting' (15). This task of patiently paying attention is assumed by Didion when explaining her creative process for writing about California, which was the 'spiritually seismic' example of 'an artist's eye looking at my home' that inspired Gerwig to make *Lady Bird* (quoted in Dercksen 2018). Didion copies Weil's dictum that 'attention consists of suspending our thought, leaving it detached, empty, and ready to be penetrated by the object' (Weil [1951] 2009: 62) in her preface to 'Slouching towards Bethlehem' where she describes adopting the viewpoint of a bird of prey above her subject, the cities of California, and being alive to their every movement:

> The falcon which does not hear the falconer, the gaze blank and pitiless as the sun; those have been my points of reference, the only images against which much of what I was seeing and hearing and thinking seemed to make any pattern.
>
> ([1968] 2006: 5)

Reticence can also pass for patience, however, and confuse the matter of which came first: was Weil reluctant to engage in Catholic ritual or did she simply wish to observe it? Was it Didion's fascination with the hedonism of San Francisco or her objective concern for its consequences that she prioritised? The dilemma is noted by Didion, who uses 'Slouching towards Bethlehem' as the title of an essay on the Haight-Ashbury district of San Francisco that 'was the first time I had dealt directly and flatly with the evidence of atomization, the proof that things fall apart' ([1968] 2006: 5). Thus, while paying attention and love might be the same thing, they may also lead to awareness of ageing, decay and dissolution, albeit as part of the natural order and sometimes as a result of outside forces like AIDS and other illnesses, economic deprivation and governmental neglect.

Lady Bird's apprenticeship to this learned strategy of patient observation is both a moral component of her self-determination and an ethical strategy of her possible creativity. This method of looking, loving and thereby self-determining oneself is congruent with Transcendentalism and Weil and present too in the modus operandi of the New Journalism of which Didion was a prime exponent. New Journalism involved the writers inserting themselves into the subject of their essays, detailing their minutest observations and concluding with new knowledge of the self. Didion provides the wry epigraph for *Lady Bird* – 'Anybody who talks about California hedonism has never spent a Christmas in Sacramento' – and her descriptions of Californian cultures certainly influenced Gerwig and Ronan, whose collaboration on *Lady Bird* prioritises attentiveness to the minimalist gestures of everyday life. Gerwig follows Didion and allies with Irigaray in this regard, redirecting the cinematic gaze away from conventional and superficial ideas of beauty and spectacle and steering it towards observation of details and their duration instead. Such attention begetting love is evident in Ronan's vanity-free submission to close-ups of her face with acne, which challenge the unblemished youthful faces of so many films about teens and, as Ronan has acknowledged, enhances the theme of self-determination: 'The fact that [Gerwig] wanted to make that part of our character allowed me to own it a little bit and in a way, to be sort of proud of it and accept it. [...] I learned that [acne] can only add to a person, it doesn't take away from them' (quoted in Lalancette 2018). Thus, Lady Bird's acne, garb and dye-job attest to her stifled punkiness and make her far more authentic than Emma Stone's character in *Easy A* (Gluck, 2010), for example, where her couture, complexion and coiffure make her an implausible desert of attention [see Figure 3.6].

Ultimately, the attention given to paying attention underpins the Kantian critique of aesthetic judgement in *Lady Bird* that is essayed in Chapter 2. Didion observes that 'innocence ends when one is stripped of the delusion that one likes oneself' ([1968] 2006: 109) and this idea – that it is not necessary to like something in order to love it, not even oneself – is crucial to this exchange between daughter and mother:

LADY BIRD: I just wish... I wish that you liked me.
MARION: Of course I love you.
Lady Bird comes out. Looks at Marion with the pure question:

Figure 3.6 Saoirse Ronan as Christine 'Lady Bird' McPherson

LADY BIRD: But do you like me?
MARION: (*faltering*) ...I want you to be the very best version of yourself you can be.
LADY BIRD: What if this *is* the best version?

Like Marion's discussion about (her daughter having) sex and (her husband taking) drugs in the family bathroom, communication in this scene is relayed through mirrors, with Marion facing the back of her daughter and seeing another version of her offspring reflected. This divided daughter thus answers the faltering entreaty to perfection of the mother by illustrating Irigaray's response to her own mother that 'of necessity, I became the uninhabitable region of your reflections. You wanted me to grow up, to walk, to run in order to vanquish your own infirmity' (1981: 64). Love, self-love and loving another, in other words, are not dependent on liking oneself or the other. Self-determination occurs when a smart young woman like Lady Bird is able to love herself, not *despite* her acne, brittle hair, thrift-shop clothes, low-income family and boring life in Sacramento, but *because* of these things, finding uniqueness, meaning and transcendence in paying attention to herself. Didion concurs and explains her own feelings about her failings as she moved out of girlhood:

> I lost the conviction that lights would always turn green for me, the pleasant certainty that those rather passive virtues which had won me approval as a child automatically guaranteed me not only Phi Beta Kappa keys but happiness, honor, and the love of a good man.
> ([1968] 2006: 109)

But, like Lady Bird, Didion also pushes through this impasse in ways that are congruent with the teachings of Weil, Transcendentalism and the resolution of *Lady Bird* to achieve self-determination. Having lost this conviction of privilege and entitlement, Didion moves beyond it to something much deeper: the struggle, perhaps, to reconcile oneself with both the possibility of becoming a better version of oneself (one that might be liked) and a better friend to the current version of oneself (one that might be loved).

A Ritual of Remembering

Lady Bird concludes with a cold and hungover Lady Bird in the harsh light of autumn in New York, where her student status may enable her radicalisation and parts of the city may reveal themselves as the kinds of spaces 'that women should look for' (Bolton 2015: 48). Manhattan may even function as a vantage point from which Lady Bird becomes a fledgling writer like Didion or a novice filmmaker like Gerwig, who will look back at the time and space of Sacramento and 'become aware of dimensions that do not appear at first level' (ibid.). In this regard, her phoning home and leaving a message on an answering machine is a declaration of independence that has a spiritual dimension too, one that, to borrow from Didion, 'has nothing to do with the face of things, but concerns instead a separate peace, a private reconciliation' ([1968] 2006: 110). Leaving a message functions partly as a soliloquy, but also as an open dialogue with her mother in the sense, as identified by Irigaray, that 'introducing some "dialogues" between mother and daughter makes room for sequences generally neglected in our [patriarchal] tradition' (quoted in Bolton 2015: 57). It is a gesture that realises Irigaray's ambitions for the expression of mothers and daughters, one that is made visible by a film in which 'the stress here is on safeguarding women's identity, not by becoming a mother, or by representation of motherhood, but by a suitable recognition of maternal genealogy' (ibid.).

Lady Bird begins her message by reinstating the link between mother and daughter and gently excluding the patriarch: 'Hi Mom and Dad, it's me. [...] Dad, this is more for Mom...' She follows this with an invitation to her mother to share and compare their memories: 'Hey Mom: did you feel emotional the first time that you drove in Sacramento? I did and I wanted to tell you, but we weren't really talking when it happened.' Speaking without seeing the listener resembles Catholic confession and approximates too what Bolton describes as 'a different framework of meaning' (2015: 57) because it suggests a new, long-distance ritual that fulfils Irigaray's ideal of an exchange between mother and daughter that can 'open a different horizon [...] if we do not fix our attention only on them' (quoted in ibid.). Lady Bird recalls for her mother 'all those bends I've known my whole life, and stores, and the whole thing' and thereby recognises and locates their shared female genealogy in the hand-me-down geography of Sacramento, which is a stand-in for what Irigaray identifies as 'another' world. That is, one 'for a woman to claim as her own, or at least in which to find expression' (Bolton 2015: 48) by means of sharing memories and feelings in order to avoid 'the risk of remaining in a patriarchal or phallocentric world without elaborating another world' (Irigaray quoted in Bolton 2015: 57). Accordingly, Gerwig also evades this risk of solipsism by sharing these feelings and memories in a montage of golden hour shots of Sacramento [see Figures 3.7 and 3.8].

Figure 3.7 Golden hour shots of the hand-me-down geography of Sacramento...

The sequence recalls 'Heavy Traffic' (1988) and 'City View' (1993) by Thiebaud. It includes match cuts of Lady Bird and Marion and is shot in and from moving cars, thereby insisting upon the freedom of simultaneous female subjectivities that transcend generational change. As the sun's low rays are refracted through bridges and long shadows fan away, the sequence plays in accordance with the praxis of Weil, as if the film is emptying itself of thought so as to receive the object of its

Figure 3.8 ...are shared by Lady Bird and Marion

gaze anew in an intensely empathetic, metaphysical, quasi-religious manner that resembles and communicates love for a time and a place and the people within it. This sequence also effects the strategy elaborated by Irigaray, who counsels women 'to be attentive to something which does not appear the first time [and] look at what appears when viewing a second time' in order to reveal the relationships between things 'in the spaces between the figures' (Bolton 2015: 48). As mother and daughter separately and simultaneously traverse Sacramento, the city that is literally a 'sacrament' becomes a sacred object of exchange between two female figures. It becomes a 'dream landscape' in which the child is able to 'move into historical time' because it is a place 'where vision establishes the child's understanding of herself as part of the world [where] you move into the landscape and can see yourself' (Steedman 2005: 142–3). Furthermore, because the scene also presupposes Marion listening to her daughter's message, the effect is that of Lady Bird and her mother simultaneously remembering themselves driving and imagining each other doing so too. The sequence thereby initiates a ritual that fortifies what Irigaray calls 'the missing pillar of our cultures: the mother-daughter relationship' (1994: 112). It is a ritual that copies Catholicism without subscribing to it because unlike anything else in Catholicism it celebrates the female genealogy that they share. Like matrimony, it is a ritual that reinforces their bond. Like communion, it imparts grace. Like prayer, it unites them in remembrance. And like mass, it concludes with gratitude: 'But I wanted to tell you. I love you. Thank you, I'm… thank you.'

4 Acts and Gestures

Verticality and Transcendence

Like an origami sculpture of a girl, Lady Bird is complex and simple, beautiful and plain. She stands at the crossroads between childhood and adulthood and girlhood and womanhood, waiting to unfold at the moment that a moral imperative pushes her off the kerb into the selfhood that transcends them all. As Lucy Bolton reads *Lost in Translation*, *Lady Bird* is also a film that 'explores the Irigarayan notion of the crossroads, or the encounter, as a step in the becoming of a young woman who is trying to cultivate self-affection and self-expression' (2015: 6). Accordingly, this chapter duly explores these encounters in *Lady Bird*, reading each in terms of the youth cultures represented onscreen. It thereby constructs a Venn diagram of overlapping circles with *Lady Bird* at its centre and each circle a genre, clique, cluster or community into which the film might fit and which its protagonist might also transcend. These circles include girls gone wild, daughters of dystopias, precocious teenagers and delinquent adults, sisters of the world, queer selves and little women. Seeking commonalities that indicate a potential for empathy and allyship, this survey considers neoliberal imperatives of self-betterment before swerving towards ideas of film language that foster strategies for reading the emergent and becoming, smart young female consciousness 'philosophically and psychologically, in terms of what Irigaray refers to as self-affection, self-expression, and relational identity' (Bolton 2015: 3). Suspecting that 'the best version of me' sought by Lady Bird includes a social consciousness, a moral imperative and engagement in civil disobedience, this chapter considers the grand Romantic gestures attempted by her and the rewards of acting singly too. It reads the verticality of Lady Bird's coming of age alongside the Transcendentalist tenet unleashed by Ralph Waldo Emerson in his 19th-century essay 'Self-Reliance' (1841) and revised in Joan Didion's 20th-century writing 'On Self-Respect' (1961). And, extending this to *Lady Bird*, the book

DOI: 10.4324/9781003240907-5

concludes with a revelation about Lady Bird's acts and gestures that confirms Gerwig's film is an independent treatise on self-determination for a new century.

To Live Deliberately

Transcendentalism is a school of American philosophy and theological thought derived from 'an outburst of Romanticism on Puritan ground' (Cabot, quoted in Packer 2010: 248) in light of Immanuel Kant's *Critique of Pure Reason* (see Shuffleton 2010: 38–49). Transcendentalism encouraged 'nonnarcissistic' individuality (Cramer 2014: xxi) at a time when America was struggling to forge its own identity between the American Revolutionary War (1775–83) and the American Civil War (1861–65). Boosted by advances in the 19th-century printing culture, whereby 'access to print became essential to identity construction, social life, religious affiliation, and civic participation' (Zboray and Zboray 2010: 102), the Transcendentalists published articles, manifestos and memoirs that explored their disputes with Unitarianism (see Grodzins 2010: 50–69), expressed sympathy with Asian philosophies (see Hodder 2010: 27–37), and settled for 'Scottish common sense' in most matters (see Grey 2010: 9–26). Transcendentalists contend that it is through paying attention to the nature of things that their knowledge of the world reveals their place in it, even as their reason for being in the world transcends the senses. Their search for meaning reveals choices that have consequences: to believe oneself a moral being requires action if one is to acquire integrity. This pathway to personal autonomy and spiritual growth coincides with the philosophical writings of Simone Weil, for whom 'the links that we cannot forge are evidence of the transcendent' ([1947] 2002: 95). Weil envisions a moral reckoning for those who subscribe to a strategy of opposing immoral laws by means of civil disobedience, which is a refusal to obey or condone what one finds unconscionable, such as sexism, bias, inequality and discrimination for feminist-minded Transcendentalists such as Margaret Fuller and Louisa May Alcott. Reading *Lady Bird* as a Transcendentalist tract frames American youth culture in relation to its moral and philosophical response to the neoliberal imperatives that dominated American society in the early 21st century.

That Transcendentalism underpins Lady Bird's attempts at self-determination is revealed at the start of the film by her declaring she wants to go 'where writers [like Thoreau] live in the woods!' Thoreau's social experiment in spiritual discovery amounted to two years in a cabin in the area of Walden Pond in Massachusetts and resulted in *Walden; or Life in the Woods* (1854), which resembles a manual for self-reliance that is also an account of an apprenticeship for a life well lived, for 'our whole life is startlingly moral. There is never an instant's truce between virtue and vice. Goodness is the only investment that never fails' (Thoreau [1854] 2004: 238). Thoreau's example of self-determination puts into practice what Emerson preaches in his sermon-like essay 'Self-Reliance': 'Insist on yourself; never imitate' ([1841] 2014: 169). This praxis of self-determination, which Emerson held was founded on 'the act of reflection [that] takes place in the mind, when we look at ourselves in the light of thought [and] discover that our life is embosomed in beauty' (191) also suggests the trajectory of Lady Bird, whose arc begins in a seemingly horrid car journey with her mother that she cannot wait to escape and ends with her imagining a golden hour drive around Sacramento in blessed simultaneity with that same mother. Such reflections as are achieved by Lady Bird in this final scene were the aim of Thoreau's reclusion at Walden Pond, which he calculated would provide him with 'pasture enough for my imagination [so that] both place and time were changed' ([1854] 2004: 93).

Such indulgence was a privilege nonetheless, only available to conscientious young men who fancied themselves scholars with a leaning towards the mystical and had inherited wealth or enabling sponsors like Emerson. Less entitled was Margaret Fuller, home-schooled by her father and educated to the level at which her renown in New England prompted Harvard to allow her (the first woman) to use its library. Picked by Emerson to edit the Transcendentalist journal *The Dial* in 1840, Fuller serialised her advocation of women's rights over several of its issues before publishing the complete work as *Woman in the Nineteenth Century* in 1845. A landmark of American feminism, it drew on Emerson's entreaty that 'nothing can bring you peace but yourself. Nothing can bring you peace but the triumph of principles' ([1841] 2014: 172) and it tailored this to the rousing of women within society by strategising their betterment by means of self-reliance, self-respect and self-determination.

In her preface to *Woman in the Nineteenth Century*, Fuller states:

> I solicit of women that they will lay it to heart to ascertain what is for them the liberty of law. [...] I ask them, if interested by these suggestions, to search their own experience and intuitions for better, and fill up with fit materials the trenches that hedge them in.
> ([1845] 2021: 9)

The text is typical of the Transcendentalists in being verbose, declamatory, sarcastic and convoluted, but unlike the treatises on the duty of young men by Emerson and Thoreau, Fuller's manifesto resembles a plea to a female congregation that must be roused into believing a better life is possible: 'Frailty, thy name is WOMAN' (10). Fuller then tracks the shift of women in France from subject to citizen after the Revolution and proposes similar for America, which she denounces for 'what has been done towards the Red Man, the Black Man' (14). She concedes that 'it may well be the Anti-Slavery party that pleads for Woman' (17) and brandishes numerous examples of the belittling of women before urging emancipation, representation and suffrage, insisting that these 'changes demanded by the champions of Woman [are] signs of the times' (19). She calls on women to acquire self-respect and entreats allyship with men in the form of equal partnerships of 'mutual idolatry or intellectual companionship' (35) and she concludes by reconfiguring motherhood as a source of wisdom that must be rescued from the private domestic domain and the abstract mystical world alike, and revalued as practical, everyday advice to be followed by respectful daughters:

> On this subject, let every woman, who has begun to think, examine herself. […] When many women have thought upon this subject, some will be fit for the senate, and one such senate in operation would affect the morals of the civilized world. At present, I look to the young. […] Their service should be action and conservatism, not of old habits, but of a better nature, enlightened by hopes that daily grow brighter.
>
> (69)

Thinking for herself, examining herself, is what makes Lady Bird the latest in a long line of those who 'have waited here long in the dust; we are tired and hungry; but the triumphal procession must appear at last' (16). This procession attracts Lady Bird, charging her with realising a grand Romantic gesture that is already sensed by her brother: 'I think Lady Bird wants to make an entrance. She's mad we don't have a spiral staircase.'

Acting Singly

Emerson advises that 'goodness must have some edge to it, else it is none' ([1841] 2014: 153) and he requires that the grand Romantic gesture must be 'your genuine action [that] will explain itself and will explain your other genuine actions. Your conformity explains nothing. Act singly, and what you have already done will justify you now' (157). Acting singly aligns the subjective feminist acts of young women like Fuller, Weil and Lady Bird with Irigaray's ideas on language and its syntax by which 'the whole framework of their identity has to be constructed, or reconstructed' (Irigaray 2007: 41). Lady Bird is both subject (I) and object (me) in Emerson's dictum – 'What I must do is all that concerns me, not what the people think' ([1841] 2014: 154), while they 'the people' begin with her mother. Indeed, this oppositionality is an essential trait of stroppy teenagers, one that rightly 'manifests itself during childhood with behaviours such as stubbornness, argumentativeness, tantrums, noncompliance, and defiance' (Banks and Lewis 2018). Lady Bird's mission may seem saintly when she is depicted in profile within a stained glass frame on the film's poster, but this gesturing towards Catholicism is ironic, even sarcastic, for though she is as fired-up as Fuller she is as un-Catholic as Weil and therefore better represented by a description of Weil as 'the Outsider as saint in an age of alienation, our kind of saint' (Fiedler 2009: vii). If her self-determination is to amount to anything more than petulance it has to surpass oppositionality on a domestic level, which she inflicts on her mother by not tidying her room, and follow instead the campaign of civil disobedience that she initiates by denouncing the assembly on abortion imposed on her classmates.

Didion consigned her lack of self-respect to her teenage years and blamed her over-compensating arrogance for her teenage oppositionality, having 'somehow thought myself [...] curiously exempt from the cause-effect relationships which hampered others' (2006: 109). Yet she held onto, refined and justified this selfishness in adulthood by declaring that 'self-respect is a discipline, a habit of mind that can never be faked but can be developed, trained and coaxed forth' (112). At a narrative level, this explains why Lady Bird is 'frequently careless and insensitive, self-centred and self-righteous - but no one is more aware of their failings than Lady Bird herself' (Mlotek 2017: 159). At a formal and aesthetic level, moreover, it connects with how 'feminist film theory has grappled with the depiction of women on-screen as objects and subjects' (Bolton 2015: 9). This depiction, which might be resolved by acting singly in pursuit of a grand Romantic gesture of self-determination, is what prompts Christine McPherson to call herself Lady Bird instead, because 'our projects with regard to the world are mostly a projection, and an evasion of ourselves, an escape from ourselves' (Irigaray 2008: 219). The pseudonym is a satire of Catholic confirmation, a project to live up to and a means of escape, as well as a thicker skin for a vulnerable teenager, one that she might grow into in order to reach an adult world. In fact, as Irigaray states, 'a great amount of history amounts to a succession of episodes of our rushing forward to build a world of knowledge, which little by little substitutes itself for us. A world in which historians will be in search of some traces, some "skins", as testimonies of humanity's passage on earth' (ibid.). The grand Romantic gesture of calling herself Lady Bird is hindered, however, by what Irigaray identifies as the difference between *grande* (meaning big or grown up) and *grande* in the sense of grandeur, for Irigaray 'found a society in which all notions of being grown up (grandeur), apart from physiological development, seemed to belong to the other sex' (89). Grown-up grandeur may feel unreachable to the Lady Bird who wakes up hungover on a gurney but, as we shall see, her reflecting on how she got there, which prompts the final phone call home, is the crucial moment of acting singly that reveals how Lady Bird and *Lady Bird* are able to 'identify where possibilities lie for developing an appreciation of women as thinking beings' (Bolton 2015: 9).

The Right to Verticality

Acting singly with the aim of reflecting upon immediate and future actions entails 'the certainty of a child who has only ever lived their life as though on the precipice of becoming a person' (Mlotek 2017: 159); but this consistently defers the character to which Lady Bird aspires. Her self-determination always seems to be pending the grand Romantic gesture that will bestow a complete identity, thereby furthering a lineage of female-centred films in the coming-of-age genre that explore what Irigaray calls the right to verticality in female identity, which is 'a woman's right to her genealogical becoming, a right you have had taken from you [...] causing both your own distress and an unintentioned lack of fairness on your part vis-á-vis your mother and other women' (2007: 88). Weil thought of verticality as the movement towards transcendence, as if a superior invisible realm could be reached by paying attention, which Irigaray reads as 'women's rights to their own spiritual becoming' (2007: 88). Thus where the Venn diagram of Fuller, Didion, Weil, Irigaray and Lady Bird overlaps is the point where women pay attention to themselves, reflect upon and love what they see, reciprocally feeling self-affection as the result of their own action. For Irigaray, the self-determination of women that results is 'a right in harmony with their sexed body instead of one that denies it in the name of an allegedly universal and neutral truth' (ibid.). Reflection is a 'return to oneself' (Irigaray 2008: 230) that has no need for external approbation or reward; it is the arena of self-determination for women who must become who they already are because 'the object of women's liberation is not to become the "superhero" of a culture that now exploits us in this way, but rather to find an identity that can't be reduced to motherhood. To being "just like men," or to being good little performers, like machines' (Irigaray 2007: 88–9). Nevertheless, Christine adopts the name Lady Bird as a kind of superhero alias like that of Iron Man or Spider-Man [see Figure 4.1]. Indeed, she assumes power and responsibility in a performative manner, declaring 'I gave it to myself. It's given to me by me' on an actual stage [see Figure 4.2]. Her auditioning as Lady Bird is a grand Romantic gesture that makes a public declaration of her intention towards verticality, although Sister Sarah-Joan swiftly unmasks her:

INT. VICE-PRINCIPAL SISTER SARAH-JOAN'S OFFICE. DAY.

SISTER SARAH-JOAN: Some of the students were disturbed by your posters.

Sister Sarah-Joan, in a traditional habit, holds up some of Lady Bird's campaign materials.

LADY BIRD: It's just a bird head on a lady body or vice versa.

SISTER SARAH-JOAN: I think it's a little upsetting…

Reveal of the poster: Lady Bird's head on a bird body. Another shows her Catholic-uniformed body with a bird head.

[…]

SISTER SARAH-JOAN: (*trying to be helpful*) You have a performative streak, I think.

LADY BIRD: I think that too.

Figure 4.1 Lady Bird as superhero alter ego

Figure 4.2 Lady Bird reveals her superhero alias: 'It's given. To me by me'

Thus, the superhero actually unmasks herself, more like a cocky Iron Man (Robert Downey Jr.) in *Iron Man* (Favreauy, 2008) than the ambushed Spider-Man (Tom Holland) in *Spider-Man: Far From Home* (Watts, 2019). Beneath the bird-mask is a teenage girl aiming to be heard.

Teenage female superheroes are increasingly common, with Kate Bishop (Hailee Stanfield) in *Hawkeye* (Disney+, 2021) becoming a Young Avenger and Kamala Khan (Iman Vellani) using her shape-shifting powers to become *Ms. Marvel* (Disney+, 2022). In comparison, Lady Bird's as yet unrealised superpower is to become a singular being amongst so much conformity. Her call to action is not a searchlight or a nuclear alert but her own need to become a free-thinking young woman. For Bolton, 'this call could be answered cinematically by the move to the different, introspective form of filmmaking of Coppola, Campion, and Ramsay, and the representation of inner lives, thereby enabling a more reflective consumption' (2015: 38); but Gerwig engages more joyfully with the tropes of the coming-of-age film than these filmmakers and avoids the traumatic twists and tragedies that befall young women in *The Virgin Suicides* (Coppola, 1999), *Sweetie* (Campion, 1989) and *Morvern Callar* (Ramsay, 2002). For Gerwig it seems, introspection is peaceful and reflection is heartening: neither Frances Halladay nor Christine McPherson nor Jo March are bound to suffer but poised instead to triumph. Their right to verticality is inviolable and the films they inhabit are merely stages in their movement towards transcendence.

For Gerwig then, transcendence is a hidden trope of the coming-of-age genre and verticality is its underlying rhetoric. Verticality is not only a reaching for transcendence but a right to grow up and older for smart, low-income, young women who seek and warrant education, healthcare, equality and sometimes allyship. Because verticality values introspection and reflection, it partly depends upon a solipsism that may inhibit solidarity, but it does not mean that Lady Bird lacks capacity for empathy. It means her concern with self-determination can spur sensitivity to a range of wrongs and might therefore envy the activism against racism of Starr (Amandla Sternberg) in *The Hate U Give* (Tillman Jr., 2018) and against sexism of Vivian (Hadley Robinson) in *Moxie*. Lady Bird's civil disobedience against her parents, friends and teachers may seem cruel, clumsy and ineloquent, but her self-righteousness also claims agency over her sexual experiences and partners and shows awareness that all women's lives are political, thereby indicating her potential to realise this of other repressed identities too. Most importantly, she shares this right to verticality with several of her smart, low-income, mostly white, young peers in the female-centred, coming-of-age genre, which may seem as restrictive as Sacramento, but which is increasingly a forum for the expression of a particular youth culture, that of individualistic young women trying not to conform without hurting anyone (but making sure they kill when they have to).

A Genre of Our Own

In her survey of 'emerging-adult' films, Andrea Sofía Regueira Martín (2022) reveals a shift from the predominantly male focus of the 1990s, when only 20.7% of the genre was female-centred, to the 2010s, when 52.6% of such films were female-focused, 31% of them were directed by women, and 59% awarded sole or co-writer credit to a woman. In addition, the majority (68.3%) of such films have an 'aspiring artist' as protagonist, who is increasingly less likely to hold pregnancy and marriage as objectives. Furthermore, the average age of these protagonists is getting older with life lessons often postponed until their late twenties or even thirties, when their retardation or delinquency is becoming ingrained, eccentric when kindly put, irresponsible when not. For Bolton, such commonalities in the 'mimetic reworking of genre films [are] the instances of corruption of the generic conventions [that] produce gaps that are outside of the traditional discourse of genre definitions [and] thereby create opportunities for the creation of something new and original' (2015: 49). Thus, after separating *Lady Bird* from classics of the coming-of-age genre such as *Les Quatre cents coups*, *The Graduate* and *Boyhood* (Linklater, 2014), which effect a limited male bias to their subjectivity and prompt male critics who identify with their protagonists to claim their films' views of childhood are universal, it becomes necessary to read Gerwig's depiction of youth culture in relation to contemporary iterations of the female-centred coming-of-age drama.

For Lady Bird to recognise herself as a work in progress on her way towards transcendence, it is necessary for her to make these gaps and grasp the opportunities that they reveal. Many coming-of-age films and series end at prom or with the emerging adult looking back as she leaves home as in *Fish Tank* (Arnold, 2009), *CODA* and the first season of *Reservation Dogs*. Gerwig's strategy is different, however, resembling Jane Campion's film-long subversive strategy in *In The Cut* (Campion 2003). Here, as Bolton explains, Campion does not disown affection for a genre. Instead:

> [She] does something very different with the female role [and] the difference, amongst other things, lies in the film being close to, but different from, the generic expectations it arouses: the conventions of the narrative logic suggest one interpretation, but when re-read they show something different with regards to the representation of the woman. [There is] a gap between what we expect to see in the context of the familiar generic conventions and what is, in fact, portrayed. It is in this gap, arising out of an Irigarayan re-reading, that representation of female subjectivity can be located.
>
> (2008: 55)

To identify this gap in *Lady Bird*, it is necessary to move on from the coming-of-age films circumscribed by high school in previous chapters and compare *Lady Bird* with female-centred, emerging-adult films that have individuality and verticality instead of universality and popularity as their aim. This independent youth culture is primarily female and sometimes queer, is largely white but abhors (often performatively so) discrimination, socio-economic inequality and a rote education, is relatively poor but comparatively aspirational in ways that do not rate betterment by neoliberal ambitions, conformity or acquisitions. The films that fill the Venn diagram do not constitute a female-centred sub-genre attached to a long history of films about growing up as a boy, but a vital, separate manifesto for self-determination in relation to understandings of verticality as spiritual growth amounting to a movement towards transcendence, albeit one that is impossible to complete because the best versions of countless young females are always works in progress.

Because *Lady Bird* wants to 'go live in the woods' like Thoreau, the first circle of films encloses individualistic young women who actually do turn feral: Wendy (Michelle Williams) in *Wendy and Lucy* (Reichardt, 2008), Ree (Jennifer Lawrence) in *Winter's Bone* (Granik, 2010), Star (Sasha Lane) in *American Honey* (Arnold, 2016) and Tom (Thomasin McKenzie) in *Leave No Trace* (Granik, 2018). The survivalist imperatives of these young women may override philosophical enquiry, but each achieves a kind of grace through suffering and sacrifice, thereby essaying versions of verticality that can be both literal and figurative as they ascend through self-reliance and self-respect towards self-determination. Wendy travels north in search of work in Northwestern Fishery and learns to accept losing her dog Lucy to a better life that she cannot herself provide on the way. Tom survives off-grid in the woods of Oregon and Ree is too smart for the meth-ridden Ozarks of Missouri but defers her escape by enlistment because she finds purpose in caring for her younger siblings: 'I'd be lost without the weight of you two on my back.' Transcendence is glimpsed in the final scene of *American Honey* when Star, following her backroads pan-state odyssey amidst the grime of poverty, drug-addled adults and soda-rotten kids, cleanses herself in a moonlit lake. While the rest of her group of teenage refugees from society dance trance-like around a bonfire, she separates herself from them in a moment of reflective self-awareness and wades into the lake to submerge herself until the ripples fade, before re-emerging amongst fireflies. Otherwise in these films, transcendence is deferred pending further penury for young women whose reality does not intrude on Lady Bird's fantasy of living like Thoreau.

The horrors of living in the woods are also graphically depicted in the series *Yellowjackets* (Showtime, 2021–) in which a plane carrying a cohort of schoolgirls crash lands in the Ontario wilderness. Their struggle to survive suggests a potential for verticality akin to a 'Lady of the Flies' scenario in which violent and spiritual leaders emerge from the group, but the innate savagery that sees several form a cult of cannibalistic warriors is not that different from the canteen cliques of *Heathers* and *Mean Girls*. *Yellowjackets* even flips William Golding's satire of systemic toxic masculinity twice, first from boys to girls and then from the surviving girls to the adults they become in a second timeline that reveals how their experiences of ferality only prepared them better to compete with the patriarchal society they inhabit as grown-ups. Outsiderness and otherness are not the same for women as they are for men, for female otherness is a condition of patriarchy and outsiderness is rare in a society that expects their surrender to domestic duties. The dual timeline of *Yellowjackets* even contends that these teenage girls are as much mothers to the women they will become as their forty-something selves seem like mothers to the teenagers they once were. *Yellowjackets* splits the atom discovered by *Lady Bird* and shows that 'in our societies, the mother/daughter, daughter/mother relationship constitutes a highly explosive nucleus. Thinking it and changing it, is equivalent to shaking the foundations of the patriarchal order' (Irigaray 1991: 50).

Most frightening to this patriarchal order are the changes wrought by puberty on young women, which is why they are often condemned to the horror genre. Carrie (Sissy Spacek) suffers her first period in the communal school shower at the start of *Carrie* (DePalma, 1976) and the bullying that results from the other pupils and her fanatical mother, who insists her menstruation is sinful, triggers her telekinesis, which she uses to kill everyone at prom. Standing up for Carrie is Lady Bird, who righteously confronts her classmates and teachers with the mental image of 'up close pictures of my vagina while I was on my period' and contends that to do so, although disturbing, 'doesn't make it wrong.' In both films menstrual blood is a signifier of autonomous female sexuality that counters the usual use of blood onscreen as signifier of gory conflict between males. Indeed, 'as the mark of fecundity and vitalism, blood is a point of resistance to the logic of death and war imposed by the victory of human law. [...] Given the power [...] of blood to disrupt the patriarchal state, it is in the best interest of women to return to this principle' (Hom 2008: 122–4). Thus the horror genre in which blood abounds can host a subversive verticality in which down is up for satanic, vampiric and lycanthropic young females. The more hellbound that the were-woman Ginger (Katharine Isabelle) is in *Ginger Snaps* (Fawcett, 2000) and the vampiric Jennifer (Megan Fox) is in *Jennifer's Body* (Kusama, 2009), the more they assert their right to physical transformation in ways that correlate with puberty and menstruation. In *Turning Red* too, the release of Mei Lee's inner red panda on the occasion of her first period prompts a celebration of 'the monstrous-feminine' (see Creed 1993), while the films of Julie Ducornau also exaggerate the bodily functions that oppose servile decorum, silence and concealment. In *Grave* (Raw) (Ducornau, 2016), for example, the initially vegetarian but increasingly cannibalistic Justine (Garance Marillier) rejects shame and thrives on her inherited craving for flesh and blood, even if it results in her biting into her own forearm to achieve an orgasm that conflates all her adolescent appetites in the cause of climactic self-determination.

In several patriarchal societies 'the horror of the blood' (Irigaray 1992: 228) of menstruation is cause for the banishment of young women from the home for the duration of their period because the morphology of becoming a woman is subject to sexist and binary dogma. Yet the practice of period shaming by the Gond and Madiya ethnic groups in India and some rural communities in Nepal, for example, is only an extreme version of the cultural taboo of menstruation in western culture. Second-wave feminism railed against this silence that indicated the menstruating female was not only *not* male but an unruly aberration of the subjugated female too, a being that was 'something else' that should be silenced and hidden for the duration of her period. Conversely therefore, as in these films, the exploitation and celebration of these signifiers of metamorphosis overturn the discursive male privilege because, rather than opposing liminality, these women incorporate change into their bodies and proclaim it (Phillips 2017: 8). When metamorphosis in the horror genre metaphorises becoming a woman in adolescence, the bodily instability exhibited by Ginger, Jennifer, Justine and Mei Lee is an exaggeration of any teenage girl made to feel as if her menstruation is a shameful condition that threatens the decorum of patriarchal order. Consequently, the Venn diagram expands because their human to animal liminality mirrors the instability of the transformative process from girl to woman of the similarly therianthropic Lady Bird.

The revenge of certain young women in the horror genre informs the horrors of Young Adult dystopian literature in which ordinary young women ascend to embrace leadership, thereby illustrating the challenge of becoming a woman while also becoming a hero (Phillips 2017: 10–12). Katniss (Jennifer Lawrence) in *The Hunger Games* (Ross, 2012) series and Tris (Shailene Woodley) in *Divergent* (Burger, 2014) and its sequels inhabit dark and epic fantasies of teenage rebellion in which the 'becoming-woman, while becoming hero' (Phillips 2017: 10) is defined by her reluctance to inhabit both roles. Growing up is marked by life-threatening dangers and world-changing choices that have consequences for the psyches of these ordinary, low-income, white, young women, for whom being smart sets them apart much like Lady Bird. So they warily assume their responsibilities and scheme to get in and out of the Capitol of Panem, post-apocalypse Chicago and Immaculate Heart High School, respectively. Both Katniss and Tris travel a metaphorical trajectory for the becoming-woman/becoming-hero that aspires to independence from their oppressors and equally from their collaborators in revolution too. Katniss unites the thirteen districts of Panem, each of which is defined by a different skill or trade, against the totalitarianism of the Capitol and thereby maps a model for verticality through this metaphorical school syllabus. Meanwhile, Tris is made to take a test that will reveal her belonging to one of five factions and so resembles the challenge of finding one's place amongst the teenage tribes of the high school canteen. Both Katniss and Tris embark upon paths to verticality that end up messianic but are not unrelatable models for schoolgirls like Lady Bird because they are young women who also inhabit 'counter-cultural spaces in which alternative frameworks for living and being an adolescent female are possible' (3). In recent Star Wars films, the ascent of Rey (Daisy Ridley) from scavenger to Jedi master is another example of a smart, low-income, young, white woman achieving verticality on a par with Lady Bird getting into an East Coast college.

Gesturing towards Adulthood

The girl-to-woman dynamic of the coming-of-age genre tends towards an embedded verticality, although there are exceptions like Maribel (Stephanie Beatriz) in *Encanto* (Howard and Bush, 2021), who, having failed to reveal a 'magical gift' at her own coming-of-age ceremony, has not proceeded from girl to woman but been condemned to a spinster's life of taking care of her extended family. In addition, some films are spoiled by the precocity of young girls that reach or are pushed into adulthood too soon, while others are wrecked by the delinquency of those who hang onto girlhood too long. Female-centred coming-of-age films that essay the premature end of adolescence extend backwards into childhood with fifteen-year-old Mia (Katie Jarvis) in *Fish Tank*, fourteen-year-old Lila in *It Felt Like Love*, thirteen-year-old Kayla (Elsie Fisher) in *Eighth Grade* (Burnham, 2018) and twelve-year-old Dawn (Heather Matarazzo) in *Welcome to the Dollhouse* (Solondz, 1996), all the way back to the ruined infancy of six-year-old Moonnee (Brooklyn Prince) in *The Florida Project* (Baker, 2017). Innocence is lost to peer pressure, anxiety, abuse and the deception of adults in these films, which erase the verticality of the genre by disallowing self-affection, self-respect and self-determination. Meanwhile, at the other extreme, there are twenty-somethings clinging to the remnants of girlhood, such as Susan (Melanie Mayron) in *Girlfriends*, Ruby (Ashley Judd) in *Ruby in Paradise*, Alana (Alana Haim) in *Licorice Pizza* (Anderson, 2021), Julie in *Verdens verste menneske* and, of course, Frances (Greta Gerwig) in *Frances Ha*. Susan refuses to move on when her best friend gets married – 'I caught the bouquet. Then I dropped it' – while Ruby grows up in Tennessee and flees to Florida, where she tentatively grows up again. Alana, Julie and Frances all run when the pressures of adulthood get to them and turn back time in varied ways: Alana hangs out with a fifteen-year-old boy, Julie avoids commitment and consequences by literally freezing time in Oslo, and Frances precedes Lady Bird by being so delighted at having 'a Walden Pond moment' that she calls her mother (played by Gerwig's own mother, Christine), who asks where she is. 'Nature!' exclaims Frances. 'Oh you know what I found out, Thoreau lived about five minutes from his mom's house!'

All these women can be mapped onto the waves of feminism described in Chapter 1. Some, like Susan, Ruby and Alana are coming of age during the second wave of feminism and finding that escaping the conformity of their parents' generations leaves them so directionless that they are inclined to hang on to girlhood because 'generally speaking, the postfeminist takes for granted the goals and gains of second-wave feminism [and] rather than rejecting femininity, delight[s] in such "feminine" pursuits as shopping, wearing make-up, and pursuing (usually) heterosexual romance' (Handyside 2017: 2). Contrastingly, Rue (Zendaya) in *Euphoria* is at the seeming endpoint of the fourth wave, where the unrelenting focus on abuse, body shaming, sexual harassment and rape culture has proven so psychologically damaging that she is physically self-destructing, drugged-up and numb in the middle ground between precocity and delinquency and refusing to move in either direction. Lady Bird comes of age in the early 2000s in the gap between the third and fourth waves of feminism, which is a time that has inspired not nostalgia but critical reflection on the body shaming and fatphobia of mainstream culture that countered the postfeminist valorisation of young women like Lady Bird at that time. Lady Bird jokes about tanning with Julie and goadingly tells her mother she wishes she could get an eating disorder, but she does not suffer the 'bubblegum misogyny' (Grady 2021) of the late 1990s and early 2000s, when the 'Fat Monica' plotline played out on the series *Friends* (NBC, 1994–2004) and both 'ugly ducking' Tai (Brittany Murphy) in *Clueless* and 'sad, little person' Andrea (Anne Hathaway) in *The Devil Wears Prada* (Frankel, 2006) were 'redeemed' by weight loss. Thus there is something to be celebrated in Lady Bird having a second helping of pasta that her mother 'suggested' she not take and buying 'one pack of Camel Lights, please. And a scratcher. And a *Playgirl*' on her 18th birthday. Indeed, Lady Bird seems immune to the 'constrictive standards of girl and womanhood' put about by magazines like *Teen* and *Seventeen*, which reached 87% of American girls between the ages of twelve and nineteen during the years 1992–2003 and were read by young women 'trying to figure to what it means to be a young woman' (Petersen 2021). That said, the plot of *Lady Bird* does demand that '*sweet* [and] *chubby*' Julie be found alone at home and crying from lack of a prom date so that Lady Bird can rescue her, which would grate further if it were not for the corrective that their unruly indulgence in food prompts their teenage revolution:

INT. JULIE'S KITCHEN. NIGHT.

They laugh really hard. They catch their breath and notice that they are on the last slice of the block of cheese.

LADY BIRD: We ate all the cheese!

JULIE: It's ok, Blocks of cheese vary in size, that was a small one.

LADY BIRD: So small. Fuck it, let's go to prom.

In 2002–03, Lady Bird is shown to be increasingly sensitive to discrimination and keen to become part of the cultural conversation that was largely the reserve of activists in this gap between the third and fourth waves of feminism. The high school triumvirate of Samantha, Clare and Andie played by Molly Ringwald in *Sixteen Candles* (Hughes, 1984), *The Breakfast Club* (Hughes, 1985) and *Pretty in Pink* is yet to be disparaged after the release of *Lady Bird* by Ringwald herself, when the actor noted 'how inappropriate much of John [Hughes]'s writing was' (Ringwald 2018). Yet Lady Bird is also solipsistic and uninformed, privileged in the sense that she knows nothing of her many 'sisters' in the world for whom survival takes precedence over entitled self-determination. Lacking such perspective, her grand Romantic gestures are self-serving. While Lady Bird frets over her prom dress and getting into college, Ida (Sandra Guldberg Kampp) in *Kød & Blod* (Wildland) (Nordahl, 2020) is trying to survive amongst her adoptive family of violent criminals, Selma in *Cigare au miel* is caught up in the tensions emanating from the French-Algerian conflict, Ana (Maryua Membreño) lives in dread of a violent drug cartel and its trafficking of girls in *Noche de Fuego* (Prayers for the Stolen) (Huezo, 2021), Venera (Kosovare Krasniqi) in *Në kërkim të Venerës* (Looking for Venera) (Sefa, 2021) is struggling to breathe in a crowded home in a remote village in Kosovo, Marieme (Karidja Touré) in *Bande de filles* is caught up in cycles of abuse, drugs and violence on the outskirts of Paris, Otilia (Anamaria Marinca) is prostituting herself to pay for her best friend's illegal abortion in *4 luni, 3 săptămâni și 2 zile* (4 Months, 3 Weeks and 2 Days) (Mungiu, 2007) and Lilja (Oksana Akinshina) in *Lilja 4-ever* (Lilya 4-ever) (Moodysson, 2002) is abandoned by her mother, trafficked, raped, abused and prostituted until she commits suicide. For these young women, girlhood is a myth, a privilege they cannot acquire: coming of age happens suddenly, violently and sometimes not at all.

Expecting Lady Bird to consider global sisterhood is premature, perhaps, especially when she does not yet have access to social media. But she also knows nothing of a girl of the Oglala Lakota nation in South Dakota, or a child of deaf adults in Gloucester, Massachusetts, or a gay Black boy in Liberty City, Miami: respectively, the teenage protagonists of *Songs My Brothers Taught Me* (Zhao, 2015), *CODA* and *Moonlight*, who know nothing of her either. Nevertheless, in the Venn diagram of interlocking films about youth cultures, *Lady Bird* stands with all these films to 'solidify the idea of a "forced" coming-of-age story, one uniquely attuned to modern times' (Groff 2018). The films mentioned might not document the performative rituals of the Jewish Bat Mitzvah, Amish Rumspringa, Hispanic quinceañera, Malaysian Khatam Al Koran, Confucian Ji Li or Apache sunrise ceremony, but they each describe growing up as an inexorable series of challenges that can include these same or similar rituals. Thus, although conscious allyship is currently beyond Lady Bird and the idea that being a teenager might be a privilege or even a myth in other cultures does not arise, her verticality coincides with the simultaneity of many young women in films such as these. Attuned to modern times, these films all invert the trope of the traditional coming-of-age film that launches young people on their way towards the adult world because they bring the adult world hurtling towards them.

Swerving the Norm

Lady Bird reads her independence in terms of autonomy from her mother, who does not appear to provide her own daughter with a role model resulting from her own self-determination. Neither do her teachers, who are sexless nuns subject to faith-based heteronomy, while her disappointing boyfriends (one gay, one distracted and indifferent) barely register as markers for Lady Bird, who 'regards neither romantic breakdown as a treatise on her own self-worth; how she values herself is almost entirely self-determined' (Williams 2018). Lady Bird is a precocious, performative, solipsistic, American teenager, whose smartness is as relative as her low-income status. As yet she withholds allyship although her potential for solidarity is present in her relationships with Julie, Danny and eventually her mother, as well as in the film's leaning into queerness. *Lady Bird* and *Moonlight* were breakthrough films for the A24 independent production company and congruent in their responses to a history of cisgendered and heterosexual, white male bias in the coming-of-age genre because their socially conscious reconsiderations of under-represented youth cultures offered fresh perspectives on growing up gendered in the new century. Swerving the norm meant that outsiderness, otherness, difficult mothers and self-determination gave Lady Bird and the teenage Chiron (Ashton Sanders) something in common that might otherwise have been erased by an exclusive attention to other matters such as race. Indeed, both films connected to a spectatorship that was not so rigidly gendered nor racially divided nor sexually discriminatory as that which had, as Molly Ringwald reflected, previously accepted 'the scope of the ugliness [that] could also be considered racist, misogynistic, and, at times, homophobic' in the coming-of-age films of John Hughes (Ringwald 2018).

At the very least, Lady Bird can be situated along an infrequent but important lineage of morally conscious awkwardness with assigning binary gender roles to adolescents in American cinema, one that takes *Rebel Without A Cause* (Ray, 1955) and *The Graduate* as reference points for their portrayal of modern American youth being pummelled by social and familial expectations of gender. Like Jim Stark (James Dean) and Benjamin Braddock (Dustin Hoffman), Lady Bird is uncomfortable with growing up gendered in ways that reveal the limitations and expectations placed upon her. Eschewing the mainstream history of coming-of-age films that favours a romantic and gendered binary, Lady Bird leans into an alternative lineage of films that promote self-determination in matters of gender and sexuality and provide exceptions to heteronormativity and rigid gender roles. Romantic comedy films about gay teenagers such as *Love, Simon* (Berlanti, 2018) and *Crush* (Cohen, 2022) may still be few, but high school has become an ideal and even idealised venue for exploring and celebrating queerness in series that coincide with fourth-wave feminism in their focus on empowerment, the Internet and intersectionality, such as *Glee*, *Degrassi: Next Class* (Family, 2016–17), *Atypical* (Netflix, 2017–21), *Derry Girls*, *PEN15* (Hulu, 2019–21), *High School Musical: The Series* (Disney, 2019–), *Sex Education*, *Love, Victor* (Disney, 2020–22), *Never Have I Ever* (Netflix, 2020–) and *Heartstopper* (Netflix, 2022–). Acknowledging individuality and uniqueness is the new trope of the postfeminist high school genre, which counters the marginalisation of people on grounds of race, class, gender, sexual orientation or disability while simultaneously insisting that coming-of-age experiences in matters of the heart (crushes, rivals, inexperience) are common to all; but to what extent is a queer reading of *Lady Bird* possible or even appropriate?

Lady Bird is not an LGBTQ+ themed film and its female protagonist is only romantically attracted to and sexually active with young males. Yet her coming-of-age still entails an exploration of self-affection, self-expression and relational identity that suggests how the self-determination of young women like her might amount to 'a state of genuine sexual difference, rather than a traditional male/female binarism that has negative connotations for the female' (Bolton 2015: 2). 'It's normal to not touch a penis' reflects Lady Bird, who judges first-time sex with Kyle to be 'a whole experience that was wrong'; but she does not display, suffer or care for experiences that might align her arc with being queer and any appropriation of the term to describe the film that carries her name would be inappropriate. In her pursuit of self-determination, however, there is a necessary destabilisation of identity that is performative, transformative and postfeminist, and thus overlaps with queer theory and history on the Venn diagram.

Lady Bird experiences crushes on two boys. The first is romantic:

> *Danny stands. He's very handsome. Strapping, even. He gives his sheet music to Miss Patty. Then he sings.* [...] *He's AMAZING. Julie and Lady Bird look at each other. DREAM BOAT CITY.*

And the second is sexual:

> *Kyle Scheible, a long-haired beautiful bassist, is really into it. Lady Bird spends an extra-long time looking at this Kyle Scheible. She feels DEEPLY ATTRACTED to him. She looks at Danny, she loves him, yes, but there is something else going on with Kyle Scheible. She's not sure, maybe it's the pot. Maybe not. REMEMBER KYLE, Lady Bird will.*

Both impulses shape Lady Bird a little more and yet each suggests that the search for truthfulness in individual identity is not explicitly linked to an objective feminist reaction but to intensely subjective impulses that incorporate progressive, less rigid attitudes to female sexuality. Gerwig states in her script that Lady Bird '*wants to be part of this thing, this popular-straight-kid thing she's always been outside of*' and this suggestion of experimental, non-straight outsiderness is part of her transitional nature. It prompts her commitment to the Derridean strategy of writing the names of those to whom she is attracted on her bedroom wall and then crossing them out, but leaving the crossed-out names next to new ones when fresh crushes come along. First, '*underneath her window sill by her bed, Lady Bird writes the name: DANNY. She's in love and wants to make it permanent somewhere*' and then later '*she writes Kyle's name next to where she'd written Danny's name. Touches her hand where he'd touched it. Then touches her mouth. She wants, she wants*' [see Figure 4.3]. As a performative act of constantly deferring her identity to incorporate new differences (that can be read as a Derridean act of *différance*), this subscription to crossing-out has space on her bedroom wall for an infinite and varied list of romantic and sexual experiences: '*Lady Bird repaints her room, covering the pink walls – and Danny and Kyle's names – in fresh white*' [see Figure 4.4]. A blank canvas, she enacts this vital stage in her process of self-determination by putting herself under erasure and thereby launches herself from a springboard of third-wave feminism that 'defined itself against the second wave [and] the idea that second wave feminists somehow policed morality and sexuality, thereby enforcing binary identity' (Howie 2008: 104).

Because Lady Bird's self-determination can potentially subvert cliché, she only declares 'I actually want to <u>go</u> to prom,' when this means going with Julie [see Figure 4.5]:

INT. PROM. NIGHT.

Julie and Lady Bird are slow dancing together. All the decorations, the whole thing, looks like hell, actual hell. There are flames everywhere. They are taking pictures together and happy - it is their last hurrah.

Figure 4.3 Lady Bird builds on her Derridean process of becoming by leaving the crossed-out name of an ex-boyfriend next to that of her new one

Figure 4.4 Lady Bird enacts a vital stage in her Derridean process of self-determination by putting herself under erasure

This sororal friendship recalls that in *Frances Ha* and suggests that Lady Bird is another one of 'Gerwig's characters [who] routinely undermine the normative tropes of the coming-of-age comedy, providing an implicit critique of binary identity' (Harbord 2019: 190). When compared to *Booksmart*, however, it is notable that while Feldstein's Molly is similar to her Julie in *Lady Bird*, Kaitlyn Dever's Amy is happily, openly gay because *Booksmart* is 'bullheaded [about] queering the teen comedy' (Gutowitz 2019) in ways that render *Lady Bird* timid

Figure 4.5 Their last hurrah: Lady Bird and Julie at prom

in comparison. Nevertheless, holding that gender is a construct and therefore a key aspect of self-determination, *Lady Bird* is more than just another of Gerwig's 'incomplete and imperfect performances of heterosexual femininity' in films directed by others (Harbord 2019: 179) and the same can be said of Ronan's Jo March in *Little Women*. The novel's author, Louisa May Alcott, grew up amidst the exponents of Transcendentalism and embedded its tenets of authentic individualism in her novels. Indeed, as Peyton Thomas (2022) has revealed in a read-through podcast of *Little Women* that follows queer threads, Alcott herself was possibly trans, which Gerwig transposes to Jo's relationship with Laurie (Timothée Chalamet) in her adaptation in a way that reflects back on the actors and their roles in *Lady Bird*: '"They find each other before they've committed to a gender," says Gerwig. "It wouldn't be wrong to call Saoirse handsome and Timothée beautiful. Both have a slightly androgynous quality that makes them perfect for these characters"' (quoted in Saraiya 2019). Thus, the Venn diagram's final overlap of Lady Bird with Jo March enhances the congruence of Gerwig's films and several of her performances, wherein the threat of conformity brings on civil disobedience in 'the liminal space between adolescence and adulthood [in ways that] expose over and over again the cost of "coming of age" and provide moments in which a failure to accede to adult heteronormativity and financial success are truly triumphant' (Harbord 2019: 179). Such failure is deliberate and expected along the lines of Lady Bird's campaign for student council: 'It's my tradition to run for office. Don't worry, I won't win.' Nevertheless, these acts and gestures are essential, prompted by the moral obligation of Transcendentalism and crucial to self-determination too. The only problem, as Gerwig admits, is distinguishing between meaningless gestures and meaningful acts because 'when you're young, you don't know what in your life will turn out to be a lark and what will become something solid' (Gerwig 2022).

The Final Act

Lady Bird may not be radicalised by the end of Gerwig's film, but she is empathetic. Feeling herself alone but strong, incomplete and guilty of being ungrateful, her decision to phone home is the act of self-determination that she has been moving towards all along. Dishevelled, hungover and astray in New York, Lady Bird reads her condition as penance for having been ashamed of being from Sacramento at a party the previous night in which she had told a young man that she was from San Francisco instead, thereby disobeying Irigaray's dictum that 'what a woman has to do is to maintain an irreducible difference between the other and herself, while preserving her natural origins or roots' (2008: 228). Because Lady Bird neglects Irigaray's corollary that 'self-affection is the basis and the first condition of human dignity' (ibid.), she is '*immediately ashamed*' by her circumstances in Manhattan, which nevertheless prove by consequence that 'by uprooting oneself, one seeks greater reality' (Weil [1947] 2002: 39). Thus, this final sequence is a reckoning with her situation that skirts spiritual awakening because, if innocence and experience are the two sides of most coming-of-age tales, the essential flip from subject to object in Lady Bird's reflective process occurs at this moment when she considers herself critically because, as Didion explains, 'innocence ends when one is stripped of the delusion that one likes oneself' ([1961] 2006: 109). Consequently, Lady Bird's decision to phone her mother suggests that she is on course to an intuitive knowledge of her own self-determination, one that is encouraged by the incantation of the nearby church choir that she suspects must mean something to her, albeit secular and subdued. In doing so, the self-determination to which Lady Bird aspires is found in reflections of the kind that intercede and are illustrated by match-cuts that express a rapturous simultaneity of mother and daughter, one that fully realises 'women on-screen as objects and subjects' (Bolton 2015: 9) [see Figures 4.6 and 4.7]. Reflecting upon what she has lost and what she has gained, Lady Bird remembers herself and imagines her mother too, driving around Sacramento, and the match-cuts realise 'the ability to represent herself and her mother as two, intimately intertwined and yet of two different generations' (Hom 2008: 119). The sequence makes up for 'a lack of symbolic representation of the mother-daughter relationship and of a maternal genealogy in patriarchy' (Green 2008: 95). It represents two female subjects in deep need of actually seeing each other and it duly imagines them doing so. It therefore suggests the 'reformulation of the mother-daughter relationship [that] can potentially destabilise and disrupt patriarchal structures, and allow women to construct an identity that is founded on mutual recognition of and love for the mother as both a woman and a mother' (101).

The insight of this sequence even surpasses Didion, who 'only feinted at confession on the way to observations of the larger world' (Kachka 2011). Yet Didion, who moved back and forth between New York and California her whole life and 'has always been birdlike' (ibid.), also informs these final moments of Lady Bird remembering with her observation that 'although to be driven back upon oneself is an uneasy affair at best [...] it seems to me now the one condition

Figure 4.6 Match-cuts of mother…

necessary to the beginnings of real self-respect' ([1961] 2006: 109). The idea that identity comes from memory might not offer much comfort for teenagers who are constantly being told that they are too young to remember stuff, but the idea that selfhood is a matter of memory and that memories are unchanging, as espoused by the 17th-century philosopher John Locke, disregards the fact that memories can be lost, warped, moulded and imagined in the struggle to be oneself. All through *Lady Bird*, a smart, low-income, young, white woman seeks to make grand Romantic gestures that will make up for a lack of worthwhile memories in a place and time that she hates, when 'the only exciting thing about 2002 is that it's a palindrome.' These grand Romantic gestures include dyeing her hair red, running for class president, auditioning for the school musical, pranking a nun, smoking pot, writing her boyfriends' names on her bedroom wall, protesting a lecture on abortion, applying for colleges that she is told she cannot get into, buying *Playgirl*, having sex, and calling herself Lady Bird. All of these are memories in the making, though she does not know this yet; that is, until her final act in her eponymous film's final act, when she phones the home she is remembering [see Figure 4.8]. Then, it turns out that calling herself Lady Bird was not the grand Romantic gesture she thought it was after all, and that her infuriating mother knew this all along: 'Well actually, it's not, and it's ridiculous. Your name is Christine.' But it takes the daughter until these final few moments to realise her mother was right and accept this in

Figure 4.7 … and daughter create rapturous simultaneity

her message home: 'It's me. Christine. It's the name you gave me. It's a good one.'

The meaningless gesture is Lady Bird; the meaningful act is Christine. By accepting the name her mother gave her, she recognises and chooses to represent the female genealogy that Irigaray has been calling for. It is a longed-for act of self-determination that insists 'a change in the nature of the constitution of subjectivity and the

Figure 4.8 'It's me. Christine'

recognition of the other as an other, irreducible to me and unthinkable in terms of my spirit, could be the opening-up of a period of History yet to come' (Irigaray 1996: 110). This History is the one her mother gave her and it's a good one. Thus, though barely eighteen when she takes on Manhattan, Lady Bird snaps her phone shut and looks beyond the frame in the moment that her teenage solipsism yields to mature self-expression, shedding the skin of a film called *Lady Bird* for that of a sequel called Christine.

Bibliography

ABC 10 (2020) 'St. Francis Students, Alumnae Speak about against Racism on Campus', 6 June, online, https://www.youtube.com/watch?v=rCqKppQOQ_s.

ABC 10 (2021) 'St. Francis High School Student Accused of Bullying Classmate, Wearing Blackface', 19 February, online, https://www.youtube.com/watch?v=fRzJSCk3bdI.

Annenberg (2020) 'Inequality in 1,300 Popular Films: Examining Portrayals of Gender, Race/Ethnicity, LGBTQ & Disability from 2007 to 2019', Annenberg Inclusion Initiative, online, https://assets.uscannenberg.org/docs/aii-inequality_1300_popular_films_09-08-2020.pdf.

Aratani, L. (2022) 'How the US Student Loan Debt Crisis Started – And How It Could End', *The Guardian*, online, 26 May, https://www.theguardian.com/money/2022/may/26/us-student-loan-debt-forgiveness-cost.

Asay, P. (2017) '"I've Always Been Fascinated with the Concept of Grace": An Interview with *Lady Bird* Director Greta Gerwig', *Watching God*, online, 18 December, https://www.patheos.com/blogs/watchinggod/2017/12/ive-always-been-fascinated-with-the-concept-of-grace-an-interview-with-lady-bird-director-greta-gerwig/3/.

Baker, A. (2013) 'The Green Girl', *Frances Ha*, Criterion Blu-ray disc booklet', pp. 7–14.

Baldassare, M., Bonner, D., Dykman, A. and Lawler, M. (2020) '*PPIC Statewide Survey October 2020: Californians & Their Government*', Public Policy Institute of California, online, https://www.ppic.org/wp-content/uploads/ppic-statewide-survey-californians-and-their-government-october-2020.pdf.

Banks, G. and Lewis, A. (2018) 'Oppositionality', in *International Encyclopedia of the Social Sciences*, 11 June, online, https://www.encyclopedia.com/social-sciences-and-law/sociology-and-social-reform/sociology-general-terms-and-concepts/oppositionality.

Baumgardner, J. and Richards, A. (2010) *Manifesta: Young Women, Feminism, and the Future*, New York, NY: Farrar, Straus and Giroux.

Berger, J. (2005) Quote on cover of C. Steedman (2005) *Landscape for a Good Woman*, London: Virago Press.

Blagg, K. and Blom, E. (2018) 'Student Debt Repayment Fell during the Great Recession. Borrowers from Low-income Backgrounds Saw the Steepest Decline', *Urban Wire*, online, 16 May, https://www.urban.org/urban-wire/student-debt-repayment-fell-during-great-recession-borrowers-low-income-backgrounds-saw-steepest-decline.

Bolton, L. (2008) '"But What If the Object Started to Speak?": The Representation of Female Consciousness On-Screen', in L. Irigaray and M. Green (eds) *Luce Irigaray: Teaching*, London: Continuum, pp. 50–60.

Bolton, L. (2015) *Film and Female Consciousness: Irigaray, Cinema and Thinking Women*, London: Palgrave Macmillan.

Brockes., E. (2013) 'Greta Gerwig: Daydream Believer', *The Guardian*, online, 13 July, https://www.theguardian.com/film/2013/jul/13/greta-gerwig-frances-ha.

Burton, E. (2020) 'Greta Gerwig Has Got to Go', *Columbia Spectator*, online, 15 October, https://www.columbiaspectator.com/opinion/2020/10/14/greta-gerwig-has-got-to-go/.

Chakrabarty, P. (2020) 'History of the Term Vagina Is Deeply Patriarchal. Is It Time to Start Calling It Vulva?', *Shethepeople: The Women's Channel*, online, 4 September, https://www.shethepeople.tv/home-top-video/history-of-the-term-vagina-is-deeply-patriarchal-is-it-time-to-start-calling-it-vulva/.

Cornish, A. (2018) 'Director Greta Gerwig on the Parallels between Her Life and *Lady Bird*', *NPR*', online, 19 February, https://www.npr.org/2018/02/19/587121715/-em-lady-bird-em-director-great-gerwig.

Cramer, J.S. (2014) 'Introduction', in J.S. Cramer (ed) *The Portable Emerson*, New York, NY: Penguin Classics, pp. xiii–xxiii.

Creed, B. (1993) *The Monstrous-Feminine: Film, Feminism, Psychoanalysis*, London: Routledge.

Deleuze, G. (2007) *Cinema 2: The Time-Image*, London: Continuum.

Dercksen, D. (2018) 'Writer/Director Greta Gerwig Talks about *Ladybird*', *The Writing Studio*, online, 19 February, https://writingstudio.co.za/writerdirector-greta-gerwig-talks-about-ladybird/.

Derrida, J. (1982) 'Différance', in *Margins of Philosophy*, Chicago, IL: Chicago University Press, pp. 3–27, online, https://web.stanford.edu/class/history34q/readings/Derrida/Differance.html.

Derrida, J. ([1993] 1994) *Specters of Marx*, New York, NY: Routledge.

Didion, J. ([1961] 2006) 'On Self-Respect', in J. Didion (2006) *We Tell Ourselves Stories in Order to Live: Collected Nonfiction*, New York, NY: Everyman's Library, pp. 109–13.

Didion, J. ([1965] 2006) 'Notes from a Native Daughter', in J. Didion (2006) *We Tell Ourselves Stories in Order to Live: Collected Nonfiction*, New York, NY: Everyman's Library, pp. 131–41.

Didion, J. ([1966] 1973) 'Some Dreamers of the Golden Dream', in T. Wolfe and E.W Johnson (eds) *The New Journalism*, New York, NY: Harper & Row, pp. 304–19 (also reprinted in Didion 2006, pp 13–29).

Didion, J. ([1968] 2006) 'Slouching towards Bethlehem', in J. Didion (2006) *We Tell Ourselves Stories in Order to Live: Collected Nonfiction*, New York, NY: Everyman's Library, pp. 1–177.

Didion, J. ([2003] 2006) 'Where I Was From', in J. Didion (2006) *We Tell Ourselves Stories in Order to Live: Collected Nonfiction*, New York, NY: Everyman's Library, pp. 949–1104.

Didion, J. (2006) *We Tell Ourselves Stories in Order to Live: Collected Nonfiction*, New York, NY: Everyman's Library.

Doyle, J.E.S. (2018) 'It's Not (All) the Second Wave's Fault', *Vogue*, online, 22 January, https://www.elle.com/culture/a15841808/second-wave-feminism-sexual-harassment-generational-divide/.

Dyer, R. (2012) *In The Space of a Song: The Uses of Song in Film*, New York, NY: Routledge.

Emerson, R.W. ([1841] 2014) 'Self-Reliance', in J.S. Cramer (ed) *The Portable Emerson*, New York, NY, Penguin Classics, pp. 150–72.

Ensler, E. (1998) *The Vagina Monologues*, New York, NY: Villard.

Erbland, K. (2017) 'Greta Gerwig Explains How Much of Her Charming Coming-of-Age Film *Lady Bird* Was Inspired by Her Own Youth', *Indiewire*, online, 6 October, https://www.indiewire.com/2017/10/greta-gerwig-lady-bird-inspired-by-youth-1201884532/.

Euse, E. (2017) 'Revisiting Riot Grrrl's Perverse Love of Infantilized Hair', *I-D*, online, 22 June, https://i-d.vice.com/en_uk/article/7xbvga/revisiting-riot-grrrls-perverse-love-of-infantilized-hair.

Felski, R. (1997) 'The Doxa of Difference', *Signs*, Vol. 23, No. 1, pp. 1–21.

Felski, R. (2000) *Doing Time: Feminist Theory and Postmodern Culture*, New York, NY: New York University Press.

Fiedler, L.A. (2009) 'Introduction', in S. Weil (2009) *Waiting for God*, New York, NY: Harper Perennial, pp. vii–xxxiv.

Fuller, M. ([1845] 2021) *Woman in the Nineteenth Century*, Great Britain: Amazon.

Gardner, R., Lawton, D. and Cairns, J. (eds) (2005) *Faith Schools: Consensus or Conflict*, New York, NY: Routledge.

Gerwig, G. (2017) *Lady Saints and Mystics, A24 Zine, No. 4*, New York, NY: A24.

Gerwig. G. (2021) *Lady Bird Screenplay Book*, New York, NY: A24.

Gerwig, G. (2022) 'Girlfriends', in 'The Female Gaze: 100 Overlooked Films Directed by Women', *Sight and Sound*, online, 2 January, https://www.bfi.org.uk/sight-and-sound/female-gaze-100-overlooked-films-directed-by-women?fbclid=IwAR0dcSyY0JsqEHdK5FYujqzdMCXfDtnENUq22SnmJ-Wb5TghfFCd2qBs8iw.

Gill, R. (2007) 'Postfeminist Media Culture: Elements of a Sensibility', *European Journal of Cultural Studies*, Vol. 10, No. 2, pp. 147–66.

Grady, C. (2021) 'The Bubblegum Misogyny of 2000s Pop Culture: How We Destroyed Girls 20 Years Ago – And Why We're Just Starting to Second-Guess It', *Vox*, online, 25 May, https://www.vox.com/culture/22350286/2000s-pop-culture-misogyny-britney-spears-janet-jackson-whitney-houston-monica-lewinsky.

Green, M. (2008) 'The Maternal Order Read through Luce Irigaray in the Work of Diamela Eltit', in L. Irigaray and M. Green (eds) *Luce Irigaray: Teaching*, London: Continuum, pp. 93–102.

Grey, R. (2010) 'Enlightenment and Scottish Common Sense Philosophy', in J. Myerson, S. Harbert Petrulionis and L. Dassow Walls (eds) *The Oxford Handbook of Transcendentalism*, Oxford: Oxford University Press, pp. 9–26.

Grodzins, D. (2010) 'Unitarianism', in J. Myerson, S. Harbert Petrulionis and L. Dassow Walls (eds) *The Oxford Handbook of Transcendentalism*, Oxford: Oxford University Press, pp. 50–69.

Groff, B. (2018) '*Lady Bird* Was Snubbed by the Oscars, But It's a Historic Coming of Age Movie', *Indiewire*, online, 9 March, https://www.indiewire.com/2018/03/lady-bird-the-florida-project-coming-of-age-movies-oscars-1201936864/.

Gross, T. (2017) 'Greta Gerwig Explores Mother-Daughter Love (and Angst) in *Lady Bird*', *NPR*, online, 16 November, https://web.archive.org/web/20200801070316/https://www.npr.org/transcripts/564579012?storyId=564579012%3FstoryId%3D564579012.

Guernsey, D. (2017) 'Removing Catholic School's Statues May Be Necessary', *Catholic News Agency*, 6 September, online, https://www.catholicnewsagency.com/column/53819/removing-catholic-schools-statues-may-be-necessary.

Gutowitz, J. (2019) '*Booksmart* Is Queering the Teen Comedy', *Them*, online, 24 May, https://www.them.us/story/booksmart-gay-lesbian-sex-scene.

Halsall, P. (1998) 'The Declaration of Sentiments, Seneca Falls Conference, 1848', *Modern History Sourcebook*, Fordham University, November, online, https://sourcebooks.fordham.edu/mod/senecafalls.asp.

Handyside, F. (2017) *Sofia Coppola: A Cinema of Girlhood*, London: I B Tauris.

Hanson, M. (2022) 'How Many People Have Student Loans?', *Education Data Initiative*, online, 25 May, https://educationdata.org/how-many-people-have-student-loans.

Harbord, J. (2019) 'Greta Gerwig's Gestures: Agamben in the Land of Stardom', *Film-Philosophy*, Vol. 23, pp. 177–93.

Harvey, S. (2017) '*Lady Bird*: Greta Gerwig on Why a Screenwriter's Job Is to Listen as Much as to Write', *No Film School*, online, 10 October, https://nofilmschool.com/2017/10/finding-home-greta-gerwigs-feature-debut-lady-bird.

Hass, N. (2013) 'How Do You Get Poor Kids to Apply to Great Colleges?: Caroline Hoxby and Her Team of Researchers are Revolutionizing the Way the Best Colleges Reach Out to Talented Low-income Students, *Smithsonian Magazine*, online, https://www.smithsonianmag.com/innovation/how-do-you-get-poor-kids-to-apply-to-great-colleges-180947642/.

Hodder. A. (2010) 'Asian Influences', in J. Myerson, S. Harbert Petrulionis and L. Dassow Walls (eds) *The Oxford Handbook of Transcendentalism*, Oxford: Oxford University Press, pp. 27–37.

Hom, S.L. (2008) 'Disinterring the Divine Law: Rediscovering Female Genealogy in the Rites of Death', in L. Irigaray and M. Green (eds) *Luce Irigaray: Teaching*, London: Continuum, pp. 115–26.

Howie, G. (2008) 'Feminist Generations: The Maternal Order and Mythic Time', in L. Irigaray and M. Green (eds) *Luce Irigaray: Teaching*, London: Continuum, pp. 103–11.

Hoxby, C. (2013) 'Caroline Hoxby: New Tools Help Smart Low-Income Kids Realize Great College Opportunities', *Insights by Stanford Business*, online, 9 April, https://www.gsb.stanford.edu/insights/caroline-hoxby-new-tools-help-smart-low-income-kids-realize-great-college-opportunities.

Irigaray, L. (1981) 'And the One Doesn't Stir without the Other', *Signs*, Vol. 7, No. 1, pp. 60–7.

Irigaray, L. (1987) *Sexes and Genealogies*, New York, NY: Columbia University Press.

Irigaray, L. (1991) 'Women-Mothers, the Silent Substratum of the Social Order', in M. Whitford (ed) *The Irigaray Reader*, Oxford: Blackwell, pp. 47–52.

Irigaray, L. (1992) *Speculum of the Other Woman*, New York, NY: Cornell University Press.

Irigaray, L. (1994) *Thinking the Difference: For a Peaceful Revolution*, London: Athlone.

Irigaray, L. (1996) 'I Love to You', in L. Irigaray (1996) *I Love to You: Sketch for a Felicity within History*, Oxford and New York, NY: Routledge, pp. 109–114.

Irigaray, L. (2007) *Je, Tu Nous*, New York, NY: Routledge Classics.

Irigaray, L. (2008) 'The Return', in L. Irigaray and M. Green (eds) *Luce Irigaray: Teaching*, London: Continuum, pp. 219–30.

Jones, L.A. and Shields, S.A. (2020) 'Preface and Acknowledgements', in *Wayne Thiebaud 100: Paintings, Prints and Drawings, Crocker Art Museum*, Portland, OR: Pomegranate Communications, pp. 6–7.

Kachka, B. (2011) 'I Was No Longer Afraid to Die. I Was Now Afraid Not to Die', *New York Magazine*, online, 14 October, https://nymag.com/arts/books/features/joan-didion-2011-10/.

Kant, I. (2000) 'Critique of the Power of Judgment', in P. Guyer and E. Matthews (eds) *The Cambridge Edition of the Works of Immanuel Kant*, Cambridge: Cambridge University Press, pp. 53–4.

Kaplan, I. (2018) '*Dawson's Creek* Turns 20: Insiders Share Stories behind the Music, Plot Choices & More', *Billboard*, online, 20 January, https://www.billboard.com/articles/columns/pop/8095191/dawsons-creek-music-soundtrack-history-interview.

Kaul, A. (2021) 'Greta Gerwig and White Feminism in Film', *Varsity*, online, 2 March, https://www.varsity.co.uk/film-and-tv/20883.

Lacan, J. (2002) *Écrits*, London: W.W. Norton & Company.

Lalancette, K. (2018) 'Saoirse Ronan Opens up about Her Struggle with Acne', *The Kit*, online, 26 September, https://thekit.ca/beauty/celebrity-beauty/saoirse-ronan-lady-bird/.

Lester, C. (2021) E-mail to author, 27 November.

Lorde, A. (1984) *Sister Outsider: Essays and Speeches*, Berkeley, CA: Crossing Press.

Malkin, M. (2018) 'Lady Bird's Production Design and Ronald Reagan Have More in Common Than You'd Think', *Architectural Digest*, online, 2 March, https://www.architecturaldigest.com/story/lady-birds-production-design-and-ronald-reagan-have-more-in-common-than-youd-think.

Markle Lovell, M. (2020) 'Confections and Candied Landscapes', in *Wayne Thiebaud 100: Paintings, Prints and Drawings, Crocker Art Museum*, Portland, OR: Pomegranate Communications, pp. 53–63.

Markowitz, S. (1990) 'Abortion and Feminism', *Social Theory and Practice*, Vol. 16, No. 1, pp. 1–17.

Marshall, M. (2013) *Margaret Fuller: A New American Life*, Boston, MA: Houghton Miffler Harcourt.

Mlotek, H. (2017) 'Attention, Attention, Attention', in G. Gerwig (ed) *Lady Bird*, New York, NY: A24, pp. 155–63.

Packer, B.L. (2010) 'Romanticism', in J. Myerson, S. Harbert Petrulionis and L. Dassow Walls (eds) *The Oxford Handbook of Transcendentalism*, Oxford: Oxford University Press, pp. 84–101.

Petersen, A.H. (2021) 'The Millennial Vernacular of Fatphobia', *Culture Study*, online, 23 May, https://annehelen.substack.com/p/the-millennial-vernacular-of-fatphobia.

Phillips, L. (2017) 'Impossible Journey: The Liminality of Female Heroes', *Roundtable: Roehampton Journal for Academic and Creative Writing*, Vol. 1, No. 2, pp. 8–21.

Potts, L. (2017) '*Lady Bird* and the Problem with White Feminism', *Medium*, online, 7 December, https://medium.com/tartmag/by-lena-potts-15b150fca7a6.

Pring, R. (2005) 'Faith Schools: Can They Be Justified?', in R. Gardner, D. Lawton and J. Cairns (eds) *Faith Schools: Consensus or Conflict*, New York, NY: Routledge, pp. 51–60.

Regueira Martín, A.S. (2022) 'Two Generations of Emerging Adult Themes', online, https://linktr.ee/andrearm. Paper derived from doctoral thesis 'Growing Up is Hard to Do: The Emerging Adult Film', University of Zaragoza.

Ringwald, M. (2018) 'What about *The Breakfast Club*?', *New Yorker*, online, 6 April, https://www.newyorker.com/culture/personal-history/what-about-the-breakfast-club-molly-ringwald-metoo-john-hughes-pretty-in-pink.

Rosen Fink, H. (2020) 'Going Behind the Scenes of *Unorthodox* with Co-Creator and Exec Producer Anna Winger', *Women and Hollywood*, online, 14 April, https://womenandhollywood.com/going-behind-the-scenes-of-unorthodox-with-co-creator-and-exec-producer-anna-winger/.

Rowe Karlyn, K. (2011) *Unruly Girls, Unrepentant Mothers: Redefining Feminism on Screen*, Austin, TX: University of Texas Press.

Sacramento Bee (2021) 'See St. Francis High School Students Protest Racism after Blackface Incident', online, 26 February, https://www.youtube.com/watch?v=tpEdyJQdtgU.

Saïd, E. (2001) *Reflections on Exile and Other Essays*, Cambridge, MA: Harvard University Press.

Saraiya, S. (2019) 'Exclusive First Look: Greta Gerwig and Saoirse Ronan's *Little Women*', *Vanity Fair*, online, 19 June, https://www.vanityfair.com/hollywood/2019/06/exclusive-first-look-greta-gerwig-and-saoirse-ronan-little-women.

Sarup, M. (1993) *An Introductory Guide to Post-Structuralism and Postmodernism*, London: Harvester Wheatsheaf.

SCD (2021) 'Woman Deserve Better Than Abortion', Sacramento Catholic Diocese, online, https://scd.org/sites/default/files/2017-06/im_not_here_for_an_abortion_11-2012.pdf.

Shaw, J. (2018) 'With *Lady Bird*, Greta Gerwig Soars', *Barnard Magazine* (winter), online, https://barnard.edu/magazine/winter-2018/lady-bird-greta-gerwig-soars.

Shields, S.A. (2020a) 'Introduction: This Is Not a Pie: Wayne Thiebaud and the Treachery of Images', in *Wayne Thiebaud 100: Paintings, Prints and Drawings, Crocker Art Museum*, Portland, OR: Pomegranate Communications, pp. 8–19.

Shields, S.A. (2020b) 'Thiebaud, Sacramento, and the Fancy Stuff of Art', in *Wayne Thiebaud 100: Paintings, Prints and Drawings, Crocker Art Museum*, Portland, OR: Pomegranate Communications, pp. 20–51.

Shuffleton, F. (2010) 'Puritanism', in J. Myerson, S. Harbert Petrulionis and L. Dassow Walls (eds) *The Oxford Handbook of Transcendentalism*, Oxford: Oxford University Press, pp. 38–49.

St. Francis (2021a) 'Greta Gerwig '02', Gerwig alumna page, online, https://www.stfrancishs.org/alumna-profile/greta-gerwig-02.

St. Francis (2021b) 'The All-Girls Advantage', online, https://www.stfrancishs.org/all-girls-advantage.

St. Francis (2021c) 'Worship & Prayer', online, https://www.stfrancishs.org/worship-prayer.

St. Francis (2021d) 'Dress Code', online, https://www.stfrancishs.org/dress-code.

Staples, B. (2018) 'How the Suffrage Movement Betrayed Black Women', *New York Times*, online, 28 July, https://www.nytimes.com/2018/07/28/opinion/sunday/suffrage-movement-racism-black-women.html.

Steedman, C. (2005) *Landscape for a Good Woman*, London: Virago Press.

Steinmetz, K. (2020) 'She Coined the Term "Intersectionality" Over 30 Years Ago. Here's What It Means to Her Today', *Time*, online, 20 February, https://time.com/5786710/kimberle-crenshaw-intersectionality/.

Thiebaud, W. (1961) 'Pies, Pies, Pies', Crocker Art Museum, online, https://www.crockerart.org/collections/american-art-before-1945/artworks/pies-pies-pies-1961.

Thiebaud, W. (1962) 'Boston Cremes', Crocker Art Museum, online, https://www.crockerart.org/collections/american-art-after-1945/artworks/boston-cremes-1962.

Thiebaud, W. (1964) 'Bikini', The Nelson-Atkins Museum of Art, online, https://art.nelson-atkins.org/objects/22828/bikini.

Thiebaud, W. (1965–69) 'Betty Jean Thiebaud and Book', Crocker Art Museum, online, https://www.crockerart.org/collections/wayne-thiebaud-100-paintings-prints-and-drawings/artworks/betty-jean-thiebaud-and-book-1965-1969.

Thiebaud, W. (1965a) 'Two Seated Figures', Crocker Art Museum, online, https://www.crockerart.org/collections/wayne-thiebaud-100-paintings-prints-and-drawings/artworks/two-seated-figures.

Thiebaud, W. (1965b) 'Swimsuit Figures', Crocker Art Museum, online, https://www.crockerart.org/collections/wayne-thiebaud-100-paintings-prints-and-drawings/artworks/swimsuit-figures.

Thiebaud, W. (1969) 'Strawberry Cone', Crocker Art Museum, online, https://www.crockerart.org/collections/wayne-thiebaud-100-paintings-prints-and-drawings/artworks/strawberry-cone.

Thiebaud, W. (1972–75) 'Buffet', San Francisco Museum of Modern Art, online, https://www.sfmoma.org/artwork/2019.399/.

Thiebaud, W. (1973–76) 'Girl in Striped Blouse', Arthive, online, https://arthive.com/artists/11194~Wayne_Thiebaud/works/478905~Woman_in_striped_blouse.

Thiebaud, W. (1976) 'Tapestry Skirt', Crocker Art Museum, online, https://www.crockerart.org/collections/wayne-thiebaud-100-paintings-prints-and-drawings/artworks/tapestry-skirt.

Thiebaud, W. (1988) 'Heavy Traffic', Crocker Art Museum, online, https://www.crockerart.org/collections/wayne-thiebaud-100-paintings-prints-and-drawings/artworks/heavy-traffic.

Thiebaud, W. (1993) 'City View', Crocker Art Museum, online, https://www.crockerart.org/collections/wayne-thiebaud-100-paintings-prints-and-drawings/artworks/untitled-city-view.

Thomas, P. (2022) 'Jo's Boys: A Little Women Podcast', Anchor by Spotify, online, https://anchor.fm/peyton-thomas0.

Thoreau, H.D. ([1854] 2004) *Walden*, New Haven, CT: Yale University Press.

Thorp, H. and Goldstein, B. (2018) 'What *Lady Bird* Gets Right about College in America', *Holden Thorp*, online, 3 March, https://holdenwu.wordpress.com/2018/03/03/what-lady-bird-gets-right-about-college-in-america/.

USCB (2021) 'Sacramento County, California; East Los Angeles CDP, California, US Government, online, https://www.census.gov/quickfacts/fact/table/sacramentocountycalifornia,eastlosangelescdpcalifornia/PST045219.

Weil, S. ([1947] 2002) *Gravity and Grace*, New York, NY: Routledge Classics.

Weil, S. ([1951] 2009) *Waiting for God*, New York, NY: Harper Perennial.

Williams, L. (2018) 'Youth in Revolt: Is *Lady Bird* the First Truly Feminist Teen Movie?', *The Guardian*, online, 20 February, https://www.theguardian.com/film/filmblog/2018/feb/20/is-lady-bird-a-feminist-teen-movie-greta-gerwig-saoirse-ronan.

Williams, R. (2015) 'The Welsh Trilogy: The Volunteers', in *Politics and Letters*, London: Verso, pp. 272–302.

Wolfe, T. and Johnson, E.W. (1973) *The New Journalism*, New York, NY: Harper & Row.

Zboray, R.J. and Zboray, M.S. (2010) 'Nineteenth-Century Print Culture', in J. Myerson, S. Harbert Petrulionis and L. Dassow Walls (eds) *The Oxford Handbook of Transcendentalism*, Oxford: Oxford University Press, pp. 102–14.

Index

abortion, 40, 41, 43–5, 91, 102, 111; Roe v. Wade, 6, 41; *See also* Catholicism
activism, 6, 7, 11, 12, 36, 72, 95, 102; civil disobedience, 41, 44, 62, 87, 88, 91, 95, 108. *See also* feminism; suffragism
aesthetics, 2, 3, 42, 43, 45 14, 60–3, 72, 79, 82, 91; aesthetics and form, 72
Alcott, Louisa May, 29, 88, 108
American Graffiti, 74
American Honey, 97
Anywhere But Here, 15
Apostasy, 27
A24, 2, 78, 79, 103
Atypical, 104

Back to the Future, 63
Baghead, 50
Bandes des filles, 74
Barbie, 57
Beauty and the Beast (1991), 8
Bend It Like Beckham, 75
Beverly Hills, 90210, 9
Bling Ring, The, 25
Bolton, Lucy, 13, 19, 23, 78, 84, 86, 87, 91, 92, 94, 95, 96, 105, 109
Booksmart, 26, 67, 74, 76, 107
Boyhood, 96
Breakfast Club, The, 102
Bring It On, 74
But I'm A Cheerleader, 9

California, 29, 30–2, 36, 38, 41, 48, 63, 65, 81, 110
Carrie, 98
Catholicism, 37–6, 49, 60, 78, 79, 81, 84, 86, 91, 93. *See also* abortion; education
Cigare au miel (Honey Cigar), 17, 27, 102
class, 3, 7, 12, 16, 34, 36, 53, 54, 59, 104; class consciousness, 12, 36, 52, 53, 54, 55, 57; working-class, 1, 11, 14, 15, 18, 44, 50–3, 55, 56
Clueless, 25, 26, 29, 64, 101
CODA, 26, 55, 96, 103
coming-of-age, 3, 4, 9, 14, 15, 17, 20, 25, 26, 29, 32, 44, 52, 54, 55, 56, 73, 75, 76, 92, 94–6, 100, 103–105, 107, 109
communion, 37, 40, 46, 78, 79, 86. *See also* Catholicism
Coppola, Sofia, 24, 25, 44, 94
'Crash Into Me', 75, 76
crystal, 71, 72, 74; crystal-image, 61, 70, 72; crystals of time, 70

Damsels in Distress, 50
Dawson's Creek, 9, 76
Degrassi: Next Class, 104
Deleuze, Gilles, 61, 70, 71, 72, 75
Derry Girls, 38, 45
Devil Wears Prada, The, 101
Diary of a Teenage Girl, The, 14, 17, 20
Didion, Joan, 3, 4, 14, 20, 29–32, 36, 55, 58, 61–3, 72, 80–4, 87, 91, 92, 109, 110; New Journalism, 29, 81
différance, 27, 28, 106
Dirty Dancing, 27, 62
Derrida, Jacques, 12, 27, 28

Edge of Seventeen, The, 36
education: Catholic education, 3, 26, 34–41, 44, 45, 46, 49; low-income, 95, 99, 100, 103, 111; scholarship, 33, 35, 48, 54, 55; student loan crisis, 34, 54
Eighth Grade, 100
Emerson, Ralph Waldo, 87, 89, 90, 91. *See also* Transcendentalism
Euphoria, 9, 101

false consciousness, 52, 54
Fast Times at Ridgemont High, 45
female subjectivity, 14, 96
Feminism: American feminism, 14, 89; first-wave, 6; fourth-wave, 5, 10, 102, 104; individualist feminism, 41; lack of rights of Black women, 6; postfeminism, 7–9, 24, 25, 37, 61, 76, 101, 104, 105; second-wave, 6, 43, 99, 101; third-wave, 5, 7, 106; white feminism, 10, 12, 36. *See also* activism; suffragism
Ferris Bueller's Day Off, 74
Fish Tank, 96, 100
(500) Days of Summer, 74
Florida Project, The, 100
4 luni, 3 săptămâni și 2 zile (4 Months, 3 Weeks and 2 Days), 102
Frances Ha, 50, 71, 100
Fuller, Margaret, 6, 14, 88, 89, 91, 92

gaze, 17, 66, 67, 81, 86; cinematic gaze, 82
Gas Food Lodging, 15, 16
genealogy, 5, 11, 16, 27, 30–3, 78, 110, 111; female genealogy, 3, 27, 29, 30, 32, 33, 84, 86, 111; male genealogy, 30, 32
genre, 3, 4, 15, 29, 74, 87, 95–6, 98–9, 100, 104; coming-of-age genre, 3, 15, 29, 32, 44, 92, 95–96, 100, 104
Gerwig, Greta: as actor, 50, 57, 59, 60, 100, 107; as director, 2, 13, 19, 21, 29, 42, 50, 51, 56, 57, 69, 84, 108; education, 3, 14, 34, 37, 38, 41, 48, 57, 78, 79; family, 24, 35, 41, 101; Mumblecore, 50; in New York, 14, 49, 55, 57; semi-autobiographical film, 3, 13, 48, 51, 55, 56, 58, 74; youth, 24, 27, 29, 34, 39, 49, 52, 56, 58, 59, 63, 68, 75, 76, 80, 81, 94, 96
Ghost World, 26
Ginger Snaps, 98
Girlfriends, 49, 100
girlhood, 5, 7, 9, 10, 11, 18, 19, 24, 25, 30, 32, 34, 36, 45, 50, 52, 55, 59, 71, 83, 87, 100, 101, 103; cinema of, 22, 24–5
Girlhood. See Bandes des filles
Glee, 76, 104
Godfather Part 2, The, 44
Graduate, The, 63, 96, 104
Grave (Raw), 98
Grease, 62
Greenberg, 50

'Hand in My Pocket', 5, 76, 77
Hannah Takes the Stairs, 50
Hate U Give, The, 95
Heartstopper, 104
Heathers, 26, 97
How to Build a Girl, 9
Hunger Games, The, 99

In The Cut, 96
In The Heights, 20, 26, 52, 53, 55
Irigaray, Luce, 4, 13, 15, 16, 19–20, 22, 24, 27, 29, 30, 31, 33, 61, 67, 68, 69, 78, 82–4, 86, 87, 91–3, 96, 98, 99, 108–9, 111, 112; crossroads, 87; verticality, 4, 87, 92–8, 100, 103

Jennifer's Body, 98
Juno, 45

Kant, Immanuel, 42, 43, 44, 45, 82, 88
Kød & Blod (Wildland), 102

Leave No Trace, 97
Licorice Pizza, 100
Lilja 4-ever (Lilya 4-ever), 102
Little Women (book), 1, 29
Little Women (film), 24, 29, 69, 108
LOL, 50
Lost In Translation, 24, 87
Love and Basketball, 55

Love, Simon, 104
Love, Victor, 104

Marie Antoinette, 25
Matthews, Dave, 75
Mean Girls, 26, 64, 74, 97
Mean Streets, 44
menstruation, 43, 98, 99
Merrily We Roll Along, 58, 59, 63
#MeToo movement, 3, 10, 64
Mid-90s, 62
mirror/mirroring, 16–17, 21, 23, 24, 43, 61, 83, 99; *see also* symmetry
Mistress America, 50
Moonlight, 9, 103
Morissette, Alanis, 5, 14, 58, 61, 74, 76–7
Moxie, 36, 95
My So-Called Life, 9, 10

Në kërkim të Venerës (Looking for Venera), 102
Never Rarely Sometimes Always, 45
New York, 2, 6, 12, 30, 49, 52, 55, 57, 71, 83, 108, 110
Nights and Weekends, 50
9/11, 3, 35, 62, 73; post-9/11 culture, 3, 64
niñas, Las (The Girls) 38
Normal People, 26
nostalgia, 62–5, 68–73, 101. *See also* Sacramento

O, 29
otherness, 19, 97, 104; female otherness, 98
outsiderness, 97, 98, 104, 105

patriarchy, 1, 6, 7, 9, 11, 16, 19, 27, 29, 31, 32, 33, 35, 43, 44, 78, 84, 97–9, 110
Pitch Perfect, 74
Pretty in Pink, 19, 26, 102
Princess Cyd, 26
puberty, 9, 35, 74, 98

quatre cents coups, Les (The 400 Blows), 49, 96
queer, 10, 87, 96, 103, 104, 105, 107, 108

race, 2, 3, 12, 36, 37, 38, 104
Raw. See *Grave*
Real Women Have Curves, 16, 52, 55
Rebel Without A Cause, 104
red hair, 2, 9, 10
Reservation Dogs, 9, 96
Riot Grrrls, 7, 10
Ronan, Saoirse, 2, 50, 79, 81–2, 108
Ruby in Paradise, 29, 100

Sacramento, 3, 14, 26, 29, 31, 32, 34, 36, 37, 38, 39, 41, 49–53, 56–8, 60–3, 65, 67–72, 80, 81, 83–6, 89, 95, 108, 109. *See also* nostalgia
Save The Last Dance, 26, 52, 55
Save the Last Dance 2: Stepping Up, 52
Say Anything, 26
self-reliance, 4, 33, 87, 89, 97
self-respect, 33, 55, 87, 89, 90, 91, 97, 100, 110
Seneca Falls Convention, 5, 6. *See* feminism
sex/sexuality, 7, 8, 10, 12, 16, 17, 21, 22, 23, 26, 27, 39, 45, 51, 75, 83, 92, 95, 99, 101, 104, 105, 106, 108, 111; female sexuality, 98, 105; homosexuality, 64
Sex Education, 9, 44, 45, 104
She's All That, 29
She's the Man, 29
Shiva Baby, 17, 27
simultaneity, 3, 10, 11, 12, 15, 16–19, 22, 27, 32–4, 51, 55–6, 58, 61, 65, 66, 71, 75, 77, 89, 103, 109, 110
sisterhood, 12, 26, 33, 103
Sixteen Candles, 102
Smithereens, 49
Somersault, 17
Sondheim, Stephen, 5, 58, 59, 63, 72, 76
Songs My Brothers Taught Me, 103
Steedman, Carolyn, 11, 13, 14, 18, 31, 32, 33, 35, 37, 45, 50, 51, 53–5, 57, 58, 69, 70, 86
suffragism, 6, 41, 90
symbolic code, 27
symmetry, 15–17, 19, 23. *See also* mirror

10 Things I Hate About You, 26, 29, 55, 74
Thiebaud, Wayne, 3, 58, 61–3, 65–70, 72, 80, 85
Thoreau, Henry David, 62, 78, 80, 88, 89, 97, 101. *See also* Transcendentalism
Timberlake, Justin, 74
To verdener (Worlds Apart), 27
Transcendentalism, 1, 4, 6, 14, 42, 45, 60, 62, 65, 78, 81, 83, 87–9, 108
tropes, 25, 94, 107
Turning Red, 9, 98
20th Century Women, 50
Twilight, 26

Unorthodox, 12

Vagina Monologues, The, 1, 7
Valley Girl, 25
Verdens vertse menneske (The Worst Person in the World), 9, 100
verticality. *See* Luce Irigaray

waves of feminism. *See* feminism
Weil, Simone, 3, 4, 14, 33, 58, 60, 61, 65, 68, 69, 76–83, 85, 88, 91, 92, 109
Welcome to the Dollhouse, 100
Wendy and Lucy, 97
West Side Story (2021), 29
Wiener-Dog, 50
Williams, Raymond, 51, 55, 56,
Winter's Bone, 97
womanhood, 5, 10, 30, 45, 50, 87, 101
Work It, 74
Worst Person in the World, The. See *Verdens vertse menneske*

Yellowjackets, 97, 98

For Product Safety Concerns and Information please contact our EU
representative GPSR@taylorandfrancis.com
Taylor & Francis Verlag GmbH, Kaufingerstraße 24, 80331 München, Germany

www.ingramcontent.com/pod-product-compliance
Lightning Source LLC
LaVergne TN
LVHW010929110826
845149LV00013B/2518

* 9 7 8 1 0 3 2 1 4 7 4 9 9 *